Real Success

and how to achieve it

This book is written for those who are considering their future, and want to make the most of their lives. It is particularly designed for college students, school leavers, and others who are at a turning point in their lives.

To my wife, Joan

who has modelled *Real Success* in her life,
as a steadfast loving partner,
and set the feet of our five children in the
pathway of obedience to God.

This book is a must for those who believe that for the Christian, work is a vocation, a service to our fellow men and women, and not just a route to money and power.

Sir Fred Catherwood
Evangelical Alliance

A reflective, illuminating, practical and Bible-based guide to personal achievement written from a wealth of Christian experience. It is a joy to read and I wish it had been available when I was an undergraduate.

Neil Hood
Professor of Business Policy,
University of Strathclyde

In his day the author of the Book of Proverbs wrote a guide for young men to enable them to make a success of life by following the path of godly wisdom. David Short is his contemporary partner who writes for the young people of today who need equally practical advice on how to live life with the help and guidance of God. This is a book based on a sound knowledge of the Bible and the wisdom of experience, and I warmly commend it.

Howard Marshall
Professor in the Faculty of Divinity
University of Aberdeen

In today's world the meaning of success is measured by the level of personal material gain at whatever cost.

Churchill said, 'We make a living by what we get, but we make a life by what we give.'

David Short has illustrated the unique and precious life formula of standing on the only foundation, Jesus Christ, focusing on his teaching, waiting for his guidance and, ultimately, enjoying success and giving him the glory.

Donald J. Macdonald
Macdonald Hotels plc

It will be a help to many young people struggling with the need 'to look on things eternal' rather than on 'things temporal', and Bible class leaders would do well to have it on their lists of recommended reading. The personal touch is important in reassuring the reader that the good counsel comes from experience rather than the armchair. Finally, I should add that it is not just of help to the young. I, like many others well past being considered young, need constant reminding that God's view of whether or not I am a success is what really matters.

Bill Stevely
Principal, Robert Gordon's University

Real Success, and how to achieve it

David Short

Christian Focus

Acknowledgements

I am indebted to Andrew Fergusson for encouragement right from the start, to Peter Kimber for much wise advice at an intermediate stage, to my daughter-in-law Judy for a youthful perspective on the scene, to Howard Marshall for valuable suggestions towards the end of the task, and to my wife Joan for practical advice throughout.

Contents

INTRODUCTION

You can succeed – with God's help

What are you hoping to do when you come to the end of this phase of your life – school, college, or whatever it is? It is important to have some plan, otherwise you will drift aimlessly, and never get anywhere; ending up frustrated and disappointed.

Of course, what you will succeed in doing will depend on your aptitudes; what you are good at. This in turn depends on your genes; what you are made of. It also depends on your upbringing and your training, on the skills you have acquired and, to a considerable extent, on your willingness to adapt and develop. These are very personal things, and wise guidance may help to point you in the right direction. The important thing, if you are not sure which way you should be heading, is to take the matter in hand without delay – NOW!

What this book aims to do is to offer you some tips to help you make a success of your life, whatever job you are fitted for. There are certain principles which need to be taken into account and pitfalls to be aware of if you are to avoid the disappointment and regret that so many find.

A changing world

It is important to recognize that we live in a rapidly changing world. The idea of a 'career' is fast disappearing. This is largely due to the technological revolution, which is relentlessly taking over jobs that used to require human effort, physical or mental. For example, the need for an army of telecommunication personnel has been drastically reduced by the introduction of faxing, e-mail and direct dialling. The need for a bevy of secretaries has been reduced by the advent of the word processor.

Since this trend is certain to continue, redundancy is likely to remain a problem throughout your lifetime. You must therefore be prepared to find that the job you choose, and for which human skills are currently essential, will in ten years time be performed by a machine. You will be paid off and will have to re-train for some quite different task. This means that it is important to keep up to date on a wide front of knowledge and to be adaptable.

Fortunately, there are jobs which it is impossible to imagine ever being automated or taken over by computer. Some that come to mind are research scientists, design engineers, civil engineers, architects, software analysts, public relations specialists, doctors, nurses, paramedics, lawyers, investment bankers, management consultants, marketing specialists, film producers and editors, journalists and publishers – and good parents! The key to many professions is the ability to use state-of-the-art software to process and control information. The service sector – helping the public directly, face to face – is set to grow. Another growth area is the care sector – in particular, the care of the elderly.

In view of the changing situation, it will be valuable to get some training in a general subject like management sciences, or do a couple of years with a big company. It is important to go for something that you would thoroughly enjoy and which fills a need in society.

In the future, it will be easier to work from home. This will have some great advantages. For one thing, it will avoid a lot of tiring and time-

> **Go for something that you would thoroughly enjoy and which fills a need in society**

consuming travelling, with its inevitable exposure to infection. But perhaps the greatest bonus is the way it will allow parents to combine work with caring for their children.

Be positive

Be positive about the future. There will always be rewarding jobs for those who are prepared to work. Don't settle into the attitude which opts out of any responsibility and goes for a predictable, low-grade, boring McJob.

Aim high. Everyone wants to be significant and special to someone; parents, boyfriend, girl friend, etc. No one wants to be classed as a failure. The message of this book is that everyone *can* be a success if they go about things in the right way.

The fact is that although success inevitably depends on innate ability and the endowments we inherit, lack of intellectual gifts may be compensated for by other qualities such as a quick wit – and especially by determination.

Define your goal

Admiral Mahan, a nineteenth century USA admiral and authority on naval strategy, set out his guiding principle in the following terse sentence: 'When you are trying to accomplish something, you should first decide what is the final object you are seeking to attain – and then never lose sight of it.'

It is probably more difficult to define a final objective in life situations than it is in naval action; nevertheless it can be done at different stages of life, and it is important to attempt it. The goal may be hazy at first, and only become clearly defined later on. Mountaineers can rarely see the summit from the base camp. Nevertheless, our steps should be on the right path, however crooked it may appear at certain periods of life.

Having decided on the goal, 'never lose sight of it'. Many people start out well, and then falter and fall by the wayside. Sometimes this is because they have lost sight of the goal. Sometimes it is because they have allowed themselves to be tempted and diverted by other attractions. Sometimes, it is because they have not developed the stamina to see them through to the end. Christians are at a great advantage here, because they have a personal guide in Jesus Christ and also a reliable guide book in the Bible.

I take a Christian view of life, because I am convinced that Christianity is true. All right; I was brought up in a Christian home. But having thought about religion and philosophy for a lifetime, and read all the objections to Christianity, it still makes good sense to me. Moreover it works. It did so in my parents' lives, it has done so in mine, and it is doing so in the lives of my children.

This book has as its objective practical guidance, firstly towards finding God's purpose for your life, and then keeping you on course. I offer tips and strategies which I have found personally helpful. Not only have I faced all these decisions myself – and made some pretty disastrous mistakes along the way – but because of my involvement in student teaching, I have watched young people make choices and observed how they have progressed. If you set off in the wrong direction, you waste time and you may damage your chances for the future; but fortunately, in the case of the Christian, it is always possible to make a fresh start.

Chapter 1

PSEUDO - SUCCESS

Kate Adie, the famous BBC TV reporter, watched hundreds of students graduate from Aberdeen's Robert Gordon University. Afterwards, looking back on her student days, she said: 'I realise I have been lucky. When I look at the competition there is now and the competitive outlook which people are supposed to have acquired, just after being teenagers, it is quite daunting. On top of that, there is quite an atmosphere which demands that people are successful. The leading idea the whole time is salary. I think it is sad. There is a lot more to get out of life than money.'

It is vital to get a right view of success. I have entitled this book 'Real Success', because almost everyone starts out in life with a false idea. I did so myself. I never had any other ambition than that of becoming a doctor. After all, my father was a doctor, my mother was a nurse, my only close uncle was a surgeon, his wife was a nurse, and all their three children went in for either doctoring or nursing. I was attracted by the glamour and prestige of the profession.

As a medical student, I was vastly impressed with the London doctors who inhabited the rarefied world of Harley Street. They were conveyed to their hospitals in large chauffeur-driven limousines. They were met at the door of the hospital by an obsequious porter who grandly took the consultant's hat and gloves and called the lift. The porter then switched on the light opposite the great man's name on the list of senior staff to indicate to all and sundry that he was in the hospital. I imagined that such individuals must be supremely happy and satisfied, and universally admired. How wrong I was I discovered later when I worked for them and got to know them.

There are, in fact, two types of success. There is worldly success and there is real success. My family used to enjoy playing a board game called 'Ratrace'. The winner is the one who has accumulated most of the 'good things' of life, such as a car, a yacht and a Ming vase, without going broke in the process! That is many people's idea of success. That is worldly success; well expressed by a self-made man who exclaimed: 'It's what the world thinks about you that really counts.' That is what many people think in their heart of hearts.

Of course, few realistically hope for such ostentatious success. For most, it is sufficient that they have reached the goal they set themselves and achieved happiness and job satisfaction. I wanted to be a medical specialist of some kind. I also wanted to enjoy middle-class comfort like my parents, with a pleasant home and perhaps a bit more money than they had. I felt that in that way I would be happy in my work, and a respected member of society. I expected to be as happily married as my parents were, and to have children. Others might place more emphasis on wealth and the opportunity for foreign travel. Others again might put marriage, happiness and children at the top of the list. That is worldly success at something like its best.

The limitations of worldly success
The problem about worldly success is that it rarely, if ever, comes up to our hopes and expectations. It is often achieved at a high cost in terms of marriage breakdown and family disruption. I shall never forget telephoning the home of a delightful colleague from another city in Scotland; a man of international reputation, who happened to be a friend of mine. His wife, whom I had met on holiday, answered the phone. I asked to speak to her husband, referring to him by his first name, only to be told: 'He doesn't live here any more.' Like so many before him, he had devoted himself to his career, gained celebrity status – and lost his life partner. We know, only too well from the press and television, how common this is in political life.

If, as often happens, the attainment of success has involved elbowing colleagues out of the way and stamping on them to keep them down, the

17

cost has also to be reckoned in terms of bitterness and jealousy. It is possible to end one's days famous and friendless.

General Gordon of Khartoum, the most famous British soldier of his day, recognized that a lot of so-called success was unreal and a sham, based on the ill-informed opinion of contemporaries. He wrote in his journal a few weeks before his death: 'The fact is that if one analyses human glory, it is composed of 9/10 twaddle; perhaps 99/100 twaddle.'

Worldly success is inevitably short-lived.

Every name from Who's Who goes ultimately into Who Was Who.

There is a grain of truth in Andy Warhol's oft quoted remark: 'Everyone is famous for fifteen minutes': surely as true of himself as of others! Even the greatest of men must retire sooner or later, and retirement brings loss of power. Men who have been giants, strutting across the stage of their business or profession, quickly become nonentities, and some of them intolerable bores.

This was brought home to me forcibly when I was a student. I happened to hear that an eminent medical scientist, honoured for his pioneer work in the discovery of vitamins by the award of the prestigious Fellowship of the Royal Society of

London, and also a Nobel Prize winner, was to give a lecture. I went early to be sure of a seat .... I need not have troubled. Only two rows in the large lecture theatre were filled. The famous old man droned away in a pathetic monotone; and we were all relieved when it was over. Everyone has heard of *Who's Who*, where the biographies of our well-known contemporaries may be found. Not everyone knows that there is a companion volume, called *Who Was Who*. Every name from *Who's Who* goes ultimately into *Who Was Who*.

The transitoriness of public acclaim is seen in every endeavour. Have you heard of Harrison Ainsworth? He was one of the most famous of all English writers in the middle of the nineteenth century, rating an entry in the 1865 edition of Routledge's biographical dictionary, *Men of the Times*, not much shorter than Dickens and far longer than Trollope's. He was very popular in America, and a number of his books were translated into German, French, Spanish, Dutch and Russian. Today, he is virtually unknown.

Fame in sport is even more fickle. Last year's hero in football, cricket, tennis and ice skating is today's forgotten man or woman. Many are forgotten after a week. Sportsmen and women are never satisfied for long. If they are at the top of the tree in school or college, they have to keep it up; otherwise they are dubbed 'has beens'. If they are the best in the county, they want to be the best in their country. If they are the best in their country, they want to be the best in the world. Even if they achieve a world record, they are likely to see that overtaken before very long.

It is the same in political life. All political careers, however dazzling, invariably end in tears. If the cabinet minister didn't become the prime minister, that is an unforgettable disappointment. Even if he did attain his ambition, it is unlikely that he achieved all his goals, and was almost certainly knocked off his pedestal at the end.

However great a person's achievement, it is never quite enough for them. Wealthy people always want a bit more money – or the health to enjoy it, or a loved one with whom to share it. 'Nothing recedes like success', as has been wittily said. Pseudo-success never satisfies.

The element of 'luck'

Unreal success usually contains a large ingredient of 'luck'. My most memorable experience illustrates this. It was mid-morning, and I was visiting my patients in the Aberdeen Royal Infirmary, when a nurse brought a message to say I was wanted on the telephone. It was the general practitioner based at Ballater, forty miles away in the country. Could I go out immediately to see an emergency? My own car was being serviced, but I managed to borrow another.

On arrival at the doctor's home, his daughter

welcomed me with the words: 'Did Daddy tell you who the patient was?' No. Daddy had not told me who the patient was. In fact, it was a member of the British royal family! He was a school boy at the time, and had been taken ill whilst camping in the grounds of Balmoral Castle.

I found the patient lying on a camp bed looking quite unwell. He clearly needed hospital care, so I admitted him to a private hospital in Aberdeen. My face was on national television that night, and in many of the newspapers the next morning.

Nothing recedes like success

A few days later, I met the Queen when she came up to visit him. Extraordinary success! But there is an interesting twist to the tale. I later learned that the general practitioner had originally asked a more senior consultant to come out, but he had not been able to do so. I was only his second choice!

I call this pseudo-success, because it was based on 'luck'. I was not really the best physician in Aberdeen. A number of my colleagues could have dealt with the situation just as well, if not better; but I got the credit!

Jesus once told a brilliant story about a successful farmer. He was prosperous and becoming more prosperous year by year. He planned shrewdly for expansion; pulling down barns that had become too small and replacing them with larger ones. Then he planned to relax and enjoy his prosperity. He said to himself: 'You have plenty of good things laid up for many years. Take life easy; eat, drink and be merry.' He thought that the enjoyment of his prosperity could be taken for granted. He did not realize that he owed it to God's blessing on his labours – nor that God could take it away at any moment. But that is, in fact, what happened. The story ends: 'But God said to him: "You fool! This very night your life will be demanded from you. Then who will get what you have prepared for yourself?"' Jesus added: 'This is how it will be with anyone who stores up things for himself but is not rich towards God.'[1]

That is the nub of the problem of worldly success. It is selfish and transient and ultimately disappointing. So what is real success?

Reference
1. Luke 12:16-21

Chapter 2

REAL SUCCESS

If worldly success is superficial, illusory and transient, real success is profound, substantial and lasting. But it may not be recognized in one's lifetime. It is interesting to reflect that many great men and women of the past, individuals who are now acknowledged as having been supremely successful in the sense of enriching society by solid achievement, were regarded as failures in their lifetime and lived in poverty. Many of the greatest musicians, poets, painters, and architects – whose art has given pleasure to millions down the centuries – never achieved success in the sense of fame or wealth whilst they were alive. Many, like Van Gogh, whose paintings now sell for an astronomical sum, died impoverished and unrecognized. So real success should be thought of, not in terms of how our fallible contemporaries think of us, but in terms of the verdict of history. This is a test which turns a lot of our current values upside down.

Even posterity is not an absolutely reliable measure of success. Just as there are fashions in art appreciation, so there are in every other field. When a famous man or woman dies, their obituary is often extravagant in praise. But in the years that follow their faults come to the surface and their reputation is sullied. Only later does a more balanced assessment emerge. There is a good example of this in the case of Thomas Wentworth, first Earl of Strafford, adviser to King Charles I, and one of the most powerful men in the realm. Miss C. V. Wedgwood wrote a scholarly and much admired biography of him in 1935, presenting a picture of a great administrator of massive personal integrity, whose unswerving rules were loyalty to his King and justice to the people. It was only after the publication of this biography that Strafford's correspondence came to light, tarnishing his reputation – three hundred years after his death! As a result of this revelation, Miss Wedgwood was forced to change her views and, in a revised biography, admit that Strafford was vainglorious, often guilty of sharp practice, and always on the look-out for opportunities of self-enrichment through political power. Our newspaper reporters never cease to remind us that many of those in public life, who are admired and honoured, have feet of clay.

The true yardstick of success

If real success cannot be measured by wealth and honours or the esteem of our contemporaries, and if it cannot even be assessed reliably by posterity, how can it be measured? Is there an absolute criterion of success? What we are really asking is: Can we discover what constitutes success on God's scale of values? Fortunately, we don't need to speculate, because Jesus made it absolutely clear. He said to his disciples, when he caught them discussing precedence – who would be first in Christ's coming kingdom – 'If one of you wants to be great, he must be the servant of the rest; and if one of you wants to be first, he must be the slave of all'. He proceeded to offer his own attitude as an example: 'Even the Son of Man [Jesus' name for himself] did not come to be served; he came to serve and to give his life to redeem many people.'[1] So there it is, straight from the lips of the unique Son of God himself: 'If one of you wants to be great, he must be the servant of the rest.' Real success is measured by service.

This might be taken as a charter for 'do-gooders'. Pick a need that you would like to meet, then go ahead and meet it. But it is not quite like that. God doesn't look for any service we might choose, but specifically for service along the line of his will for us. Even Jesus, God's Son, did not choose his line of service. He often emphasized that his goal in life was to do his Father's will: 'I seek not to please myself but him who sent me;'[2] and again, most movingly and impressively, in the Garden of Gethsemane, on the eve of his crucifixion: 'Not my will, but yours be done.'[3] God looks for a similar attitude in us, his people. The apostle Paul says: 'We are God's workmanship, created in Christ Jesus to do good works, which God prepared in advance for us to do.'[4]

The Bible teaches clearly that God is working his purpose out in the world, and that nothing can stop him or frustrate his purpose. 'He does as he pleases with the powers of heaven and the peoples of the earth. No-one can hold back his hand or say to him: "What have you done?"'[5] If this is so, it follows that those who work along the line of God's purpose will achieve real success, and those who work against it will fail.

Real success is measured by service

The Bible also teaches that God has endowed us, his creatures, with just those faculties which will enable us to play our part in his purpose. The Christian believes that the God who made us has a purpose for each of us to fulfil; one in which we shall be truly successful and happy. He has made us as we are, and fitted each of us to play a specific role in the world he has made, and which he is guiding to its perfect conclusion. The ideal is for us to see our job in life as a vocation; something God has called us to do. Real success is the fulfilment of our God-given endowment.

We must be prepared to accept that serving God along the line of his will for us is unlikely to be counted success by the world's standard. After all, the life of Jesus appeared to be an utter failure. But it was because he was obedient to God's will – obedient even to death on a cross – that 'God raised him to the heights and bestowed on him the name above all names.'[6]

We must be happy to allow God to be the judge of the success or failure of our endeavours. It does not matter ultimately what our peers, or posterity, think of us; the real test is what God thinks. For some, his will may be a prominent job. God said

> Those who work along the line of God's purpose will achieve real success, and those who work against it will fail.

to Eli, Israel's priest: 'Those who honour me I will honour.'[7] I believe this honour is principally in the world to come; but sometimes it is earthly, and visible. Daniel was honoured by being made prime minister of Babylon in the days of the ancient Medo-Persian empire. The seventh Earl of Shaftesbury is still honoured today as the outstanding architect of social reform in nine-teenth-century England.

We must not fall into the trap of serving God for what we can get out of it materially. It is easy to lose sight of 'treasure in heaven' and go for 'treasure on earth' which, as Jesus emphasized, is impermanent and ultimately disappointing.

I think of a fellow medical student of mine in

Bristol. He wasn't an outstanding student, but he qualified as a doctor with a good degree and there is no doubt that he could have done well and made a very comfortable life for himself if that was what he wanted. Instead he went to work in a leprosy hospital in India, where facilities were poor, the electricity supply was unreliable, assistants were untrained, the climate was exhausting, sanitation was poor, tropical diseases were rife, and one of his own children was to die from dysentery. He gave the best medical treatment possible in the circumstances, and introduced tendon transplants to restore function in hands and feet and faces disfigured by leprosy. His name cannot be found in *Who's Who*, but hundreds thank God that he came to their aid. In any realistic reckoning, his life must surely be regarded as a real success.

Real success is not a matter of transient fame, but eternal glory. As the apostle John put it: 'The world and its desires pass away, but the man who does the will of God lives for ever.'[8] To obtain God's 'Well done, good and faithful servant'[9] is the ultimate accolade. Many who see themselves as failures will receive this honour.

The choice
A good question to ask yourself is: 'What is the thing I want most of all in life?' Going for real success may involve being prepared to forego

worldly success. Moses faced the choice between worldly success and real success. He was a prince in the Pharaoh's palace, and may even have been in line for the throne of Egypt. But God called him to sacrifice this position in order to lead the Israelite slaves to the Promised Land. We are told: 'He regarded disgrace for the sake of Christ as of greater value than the treasures of Egypt, because he was looking ahead to his reward.'[10]

Saul of Tarsus faced a similar choice when he became a Christian. He had a lot going for him in the academic world of his day, but he reckoned it all as 'rubbish' by comparison with following Christ, and receiving God's top award in the life to come.[11] His first question after his conversion was: 'What shall I do, Lord?'[12] So, if we want real success, we must first be convinced in our minds that worldly success is phoney, un-real and transient, and that doing God's will is what matters. Then we must ask God what his will is for us personally: how he wants us to use the gifts with which he has endowed us.

This way of looking at success has enormous practical advantages. For one thing, it takes away the nagging concern about what others think of us. What an obsession this so often is! Real success is serving God along the line of his will for us individually; not comparing ourselves with others. As the apostle Paul puts it in his letter to the Romans: 'To his own Master he stands or falls.'[13] The Christian does not mind playing the second violin. One of the most influential servants of God in Britain in the twentieth century did most of his work unseen. Dr. Douglas Johnson was the founder and first general secretary of the Inter-Varsity Fellowship, now known as the Universities and Colleges Christian Fellowship (UCCF) with its off-shoot, the Inter-Varsity Press (IVP). He was almost unknown outside a small circle of fellow-activists, and described himself, aptly, as God's 'office boy'. For the Christian, the only concern is what God thinks about us.

> **For the Christian, the only concern is what God thinks about us**

A right attitude to success takes away the bitterness and rivalry involved in fighting for status over someone else. Real success is in God's hands. We can leave it to him. We have an example of this in the patriarch Abraham's relaxed attitude when he had to partition the land of Canaan between himself and his nephew Lot.[14] Although Abraham was the senior partner, he was content to give the younger man first choice. Lot went for the big city, Sodom, and became an important person there. Abraham never attained a similar position in society, but he was in the line of God's will for him. He was a success in God's sight. Abraham became the father of the

Jewish nation. Lot is a footnote in Israelite history.

There is a quiet security in doing God's will which is greater than that available in any worldly task. If we aim to do the will of God, we can be confident that we shall be a success in God's sight, whatever others may think of us. In my saner moments I do not really care what people think of me. It is what God thinks that counts. I am not saying that I do not enjoy having the title of 'Professor' and being referred to as a former Physician to the Queen in Scotland. Of course it gives me a kick. But the closer I get to the end of this earthly life, the more I realise that these things are mere baubles and trinkets; like party hats. The Christian thankfully accepts any honour which comes to him as a gift from God.

William Kelly was one of the outstanding students of Trinity College, Dublin in the nineteenth century. He was brilliant in Greek, Hebrew and the classics. Instead of pursuing an academic career, he devoted himself to teaching, preaching and writing about the Bible. Kelly had a young nephew who wanted to go up to university. He asked his uncle if he would coach him for the entrance examination. Kelly did, and the young man passed with flying colours. The examiner in Greek called the student in and asked him how he had become so proficient in Greek. When he told him that he had been coached by his uncle, the examiner asked if he could meet him. He arranged for the entire Classics' faculty to meet Kelly. The discussion so impressed the lecturers that they invited him to join the staff. Kelly declined, saying that he was convinced that he was in the place where God wanted him. Finally, one of the lecturers said: 'Mr. Kelly, aren't you interested in making a name for yourself in the world?' He thought for a moment, and replied, 'Which world?'

If we seek to do the will of God, we may never be rated a success by the world's standards. We may not even make a major or obvious contribution to God's service. But our energies will not have been wasted. It has been well said: 'It is better to fail in a cause that will ultimately succeed than to succeed in a cause that will ultimately fail.'[15]

References
1. Mark 10:4-5 (TEV)
2. John 5:30
3. Luke 22:42
4. Ephesians 2:10
5. Daniel 4:35
6. Philippians 2:7-9 (NEB)
7. 1 Samuel 2:30
8. 1 John 2:17
9. Matthew 25:21
10. Hebrews 11:26
11. Philippians 3:7
12. Acts 22:10

13. Romans 14:4
14. Genesis 13
15. Coe D., quoted by C.W. Coulson in *Born Again*, Hodder and Stoughton, London, p.134.

Chapter 3

GUIDANCE

The first step for anyone considering their future is to appreciate the nature of real success and to resolve to go for it by serving God along the line of his will, rather than promoting their own prestige or pleasure. That is the fundamental principle. The next step is to find out what God's purpose is for us personally. That is the application. We do this by considering our innate abilities – what we enjoy doing – our opportunities, and so on; and by asking for God's help in making wise decisions and for his over-ruling in our lives.

The need to make far-reaching choices faces us from senior school onwards. One of the first major decisions we have to make is which subjects we shall take. This is difficult if, as often happens, we do not yet know what sort of career we are aiming for. As we reach the end of our time at school, choices come at us thick and fast. Shall I go straight into a job, or shall I take time out, or shall I go for higher education? If it is the latter, what college or university shall I apply to? In what order shall I list my preferences? Once in college, fresh choices confront us. Shall I take out a loan; if so, how big a loan? Shall I live in

35

hall or in digs, or shall I try to buy a flat? Later, there may be the question: Shall I go for an extra honours year?

As we move into adulthood, further questions arise. What about a job overseas? Am I called to be a missionary? Whom shall I marry? What about holiday plans? These, or similar important choices, face every young adult early in his or her career, and similar choices recur from time to time throughout life. So it is important to learn early on how to make good decisions.

Often, there are a lot of imponderables. We don't know which path will lead somewhere and which will prove to be a dead-end. What sort of qualifications will be in demand when I finish my course? Which jobs offering many openings now will have become saturated by the time I am ready to apply?

God's promise of guidance

The person who is not a believer in a personal God has to rely on his or her native wit, plus the advice of parents, teachers and friends, and the relevant publications. Christians by no means ignore these helps, but they have an enormous advantage over their agnostic peers. Firstly, they have the knowledge that God is in control of all that goes on in the world. They know that events are not governed by Fate, as so many believe, but by the hand of an all-wise, all-powerful and loving heavenly Father.

Christians also have the assurance that God's plan extends to the details of their lives and the decisions they have to make. There are very specific promises of guidance in God's Word, the Bible. We have statements such as: 'He guides the humble in what is right and teaches them his way;'[1] 'In all your ways acknowledge him, and he will make your paths straight;'[2] and 'If any of you lacks wisdom, he should ask God, who gives generously to all without finding fault, and it will be given to him.'[3] From these, and many similar promises, we can be confident that God is willing to guide us, and will do so if we are humble, if we put him first in our lives, and if we ask for his help.

We can be confident that God is willing to guide us

A young friend of mine came to me to discuss a job which had come up in his field, and for which he was considering applying. It would give him promotion, but it was a long way from his family, and he wondered whether it would be the 'right' job. I gave him the promise from the book of Proverbs which I have quoted above – 'In all your ways acknowledge him, and he will make your paths straight.' I pointed out that if he was really willing to do God's will, God would over-rule by not giving him the job if it was not the 'right' job for him. The young man responded in a way which surprised me. He had not long been a Christian, and he had taken to confessing his faith by wearing a 'fish' badge on his jacket. For the interview, he considered removing it in case he was challenged about its significance and, as a result, might be turned down for the appointment. But he decided that if he was to 'acknowledge' God, he ought to wear it. At the interview, the boss noticed the badge and asked what it was. He turned out to be a Christian too! – and gave him the job: I hope on the ground that he was the best applicant!

Be relaxed

Many Christians get unnecessarily stressed about guidance. They are afraid that if they make a wrong decision, their lives will be forever blighted. Jesus taught that God is a perfect Father. He desires the best for his children and, being omnipotent, he is able to bring this to pass. He knows that we are foolish and make mistakes, and need to be trained. And we often have to learn the hard way. But God never writes his children off. The author of the Epistle to the Hebrews reminds his readers of God's promise: 'Never will I leave you; never will I forsake you.' And he adds the corollary: 'So we say *with confidence*, "The Lord is my helper"'[4] [author's emphasis]. Hence, we can be relaxed about the decisions we have to make. It has been well said: 'A strong belief in providence eliminates the need to strive mightily in order to find God's will.'[5]

God has given some specific commands in his Word, telling us what is right and what is wrong. It goes without saying that if we *deliberately* choose some course of action which God has forbidden, we can expect trouble. But as soon as we repent and come back to him, he will forgive us and restore us.

Many decisions do not involve definite right or wrong. In such situations, I believe, we simply need wisdom to make good decisions. One of the issues which looms large for young people is that of marriage. How can we be sure we don't marry

---

What we should be seeking for is a wise decision within the moral will of God

---

Mr. Wrong? The apostle Paul is remarkably relaxed about this matter. Read about his advice in 1 Corinthians 7. In the exceptional circumstances prevailing in Corinth at the time he was writing, Paul was convinced that, as a rule, the single state was preferable; but he said: 'If you do marry, you have not sinned.'[6] It was not an issue of right or wrong. He does lay down one definite condition, however; the partner 'must belong to the Lord.'

Similarly, Paul seems to reflect this sense of being relaxed about the matter of jobs and promotion when he says in the same chapter: 'Each one should remain in the situation he was in when God called him. Were you a slave when you were called? Don't let it trouble you – although if you can gain your freedom, do so.'[7] Again, it was not a matter of right or wrong.

Likewise, with regard to an invitation to share a meal with a non-Christian. Should you accept or decline? Paul says, in effect: 'If you want to go, go. It is not a big deal. Be relaxed.'[8] He takes it for granted that if you go, it will be with the object of being a blessing to your host.

Some people get uptight about such decisions as which side of the street to walk down, on the ground that an important 'chance' encounter may depend on our choice. My answer is to commit each day into God's hand, and then use common sense.

The emphasis of God's Word seems to be on an instructed mind so that we can make truly wise decisions. God says: 'I will instruct you and teach you in the way you should go; ... Do not be like the horse or the mule, which have no understanding.'[9] And Paul says to the Philippian Christians: 'This is my prayer: that your love may abound more and more in knowledge and depth of insight, so that you may be able to discern what is best.'[10] The words 'teach', 'understanding', 'knowledge', 'insight' and 'discern' seem to point clearly to the use of our minds. Garry Friesen, in his valuable book, *Decision Making and the Will of God*, sums it up by saying that when we face a dilemma, what we should be seeking for is 'a wise decision within the moral will of God'.[11]

How should a Christian proceed in decision-making?

1. *Pray – right from the start*

It always amazes me when I recall how long I used to wrestle with a problem before making it a specific matter for prayer. It is important to recognize that it is the *problem* we should take to God, not the solution: not 'Lord, give me this job, which seems so ideal', but 'Lord, you know what is best for me and what will make me most useful in your service; please give me that.'

As we pray, we should be looking for the answer. It may well be something quite different from what we expected. God always has surprises up his sleeve. We should pray with confidence, based on God's promises. And we should pray for a willingness to do God's will.

George Muller had an unrivalled experience of God's power to answer prayer. He was a wild and godless young German, born in the nineteenth century. After his conversion, he came to Britain, settled in Bristol, and opened an orphanage. He resolved, from the start, to make no appeals for money. In time, the number of orphans increased to 2,000, but he remained true to his principles and never told a soul outside about his needs. On fifty occasions, the orphanage started the day without sufficient food for the day. Each time, Muller and his staff simply took the need to God in prayer, and invariably God met their need. So what is the secret of answered prayer?

Muller set out five Biblical conditions. The first was that we must pray according to God's will, not ours. The second was that we must pray 'in the name of Jesus'; that is depending on his merits, not our own. Thirdly, we must pray in

---

Pray for a willingness to do God's will

---

faith: faith both in God's power and in his willingness to hear us. Fourthly, we must harbour no conscious sin: 'If I regard iniquity in my heart, the Lord will not hear me.'[12] Fifthly, and finally, we must continue to wait upon God until the answer comes. God often delays answering our prayers to test our faith, our patience and our earnestness.

2. *Soak yourself in God's Word*

We must not consciously disobey God's laws if we really want his guidance. The Bible is invaluable if we are wanting to find God's path for our life. It not only contains promises like the sample I have given above, it also shows how

God guided his servants in past ages, and it lays down guidelines for our conduct today. Sometimes, the Bible speaks immediately to our situation. For example, we may feel strongly drawn to a member of the opposite sex who is not a Christian; and then we come across the command in Paul's second letter to the Corinthians, chapter 6, verse 14: 'Do not be yoked together with unbelievers.'

As we read the Word of God, we should look for principles. We should beware of reading into Scripture something which fits our scheme, but which is not what the passage means. A missionary who had spent some time working in one of the European countries had run into difficulties, and felt that the time might have come to return to Britain. In his reading of the Bible, he came across God's word to Ezekiel: 'You are not being sent to a people of obscure speech and difficult language.'[13] He took this as confirmation that he should return to the homeland. This was not a wise way of obtaining guidance. In seeking guidance from the Bible, we must be careful that we do not latch on to a verse which confirms our personal wish. Incidentally, the missionary chose to ignore the last part of the verse. The full verse reads: 'You are not being sent to a people of obscure speech and difficult language, but to the house of Israel.' He did not see himself called to a ministry to the Jews!

3. Consider all the facts, carefully and dispassionately, without bias

What are your aptitudes and gifts? Do you relate well to people? What do you enjoy doing? Do you like teaching? Do you have the needed stamina for the job? (I could never have been a surgeon, with the irregular hours and night work which that speciality entails.) Do you have any limitations which rule out certain occupations? Obviously, if you are colour blind, it is no use thinking of a job like a railway driver, which requires red/green colour discrimination.

Another thing you have to consider is whether the job you are thinking about would involve compromising your principles. Is the boss honest, or will he expect you to be economical with the truth? Will frequent Sunday working be involved? There are certain jobs, such as those involving the production and sale of harmful products, such as tobacco and alcohol, that Christians should probably avoid altogether.

Another consideration is that of obligations to parents or family. It cannot be God's will for you to run away from a clear duty. Hudson Taylor, the vastly experienced missionary to China, set it on record that he had never known God's blessing to rest on an action taken contrary to parents' wishes – even where the parents might be proved to be in the wrong.

A distinction should be drawn between the

wishes of parents, which God may call us to over-ride, and our obligations to them (such as care in old age) which he would expect us to fulfil.

If you are considering marriage, ask yourself whether your prospective partner has similar interests. After all, common interests and friendship are an essential basis for marriage. It is often a good idea to set down a detailed list of the pros and cons of a course of action we are considering. My wife did this before she decided to marry me! Obviously, we must be guided to some extent by circumstances. We shall find that some doors are firmly closed.

4. *Seek advice from a wise and mature Christian*
The book of Proverbs encourages this: 'A wise man listens to advice.'[14] 'Plans fail for lack of counsel, but with many advisers they succeed.'[15] I would add that, in my view, it is often best to think and pray over a course of action for some time before asking advice from others. Moreover, it is important to realize that even the wisest advisers are not always right. One of the best counsellors I ever had was proved to be quite wrong on one important occasion. Fortunately, I did not act on his advice that time!

Resist the temptation to multiply advisers with the object of finding one who agrees with your inclination! If you ask the advice of your 'boss' or one in whose hand your future is, and he or she makes a specific recommendation, you should give a very good reason for not accepting it.

5. *Aim to reach a decision within the moral will of God*

I am convinced that if we honestly want to do God's will, he will not let us go astray. I have found the promise in James 1:5, 6 a marvellous anchor. Here it is again: 'If any of you lacks wisdom, he should ask God, who gives generously to all without finding fault; and it will be given to him.'

If any of you lacks wisdom, he should ask God, and it will be given to him

---

I have seen friends of mine wrestle with extremely difficult decisions. I remember, particularly, a junior doctor who was in the fortunate position of having been offered two jobs, both of which would have suited him well. He didn't know which to take. He agonized over the decision. He had prayed and continued to pray. He had soaked himself in God's Word. He had considered all the facts and applied common sense and judgment. He sincerely wanted to do God's will. There seemed nothing to choose between the two jobs. And now he was seeking my advice. My view was that he was in a 'no-lose' situation. Whatever decision he made, I believed that God would over-rule the course of events to bring him to the place where he wanted him. And I am sure he did.

6. *Be prepared to wait*

Don't panic. God knows your anxiety and confusion, but he often calls his children to wait – and go on waiting – for what seems an impossibly long time. This was my experience as a junior doctor on the threshold of a consultant appointment. I was runner-up for a consultant post at the age of thirty, but I did not get appointed until ten years, and over twenty applications, later. Some senior colleagues implied that I was not good enough. I often encountered the adage: 'Too old at forty.' I was actually appointed shortly after my fortieth birthday – to a job which proved to be tailor-made for me. The prophet Isaiah exclaims: 'No eye has seen any God besides you, who acts on behalf of those who wait for him.'[16] Looking back, it is clear that the job God had for me was, in fact, the best one. Furthermore, the long drawn out waiting period provided invaluable preparation for it. It also taught me understanding and sympathy with those in such a position.

Some questions

1. *What about inner impressions and super-natural guidance?*

God undoubtedly guided his people of old by

visions and dreams, and he still does occasionally guide in this way. I have met individuals from overseas, who did not know the Bible, to whom God has given significant visions. On the other hand, I know of a number of men and women, with access to the Bible, who claim to have heard God tell them to do something, when it has become clear that he could not have done so, because what they thought God told them to do was something which his Word forbids: e.g. marrying an unbeliever, or even living in adultery. It has been well said: 'The Holy Spirit will never lead you where the Word of God forbids you to go.'[17]

The Holy Spirit will never lead you where the Word of God forbids you to go

---

My understanding is that for those who have access to God's revelation in the Bible, God *usually* guides by means of an instructed mind, rather than by dreams, visions or unearthly messages. I believe that we should not take the supernatural guidance of a few special individuals in biblical times, and some in our own day who lack access to God's written revelation, as a guide for ourselves.

I have met many people who take the apostle Paul as their model, and emphasise the fact that at a crucial point in his life he was guided by a vision of 'a man of Macedonia'[18] calling him to come over and help them. What is commonly overlooked, however, is that this was not Paul's normal experience. More often he made decisions rationally – no doubt after praying for divine wisdom. For example, we are told that he 'decided' to go to Jesusalem;[19] he 'decided' to go back through Macedonia;[20] he 'decided' to winter at Nicopolis.[21] Three times he told the Corinthian church he 'planned' to visit them[22], and he told the Roman church he 'planned' to see them when he went to Spain.[23]

Inner promptings, however, should not be ignored. They should be carefully considered. Sometimes, they may be a reminder of a clear duty. My wife's mother used, not infrequently, to get such feelings about people in need, and almost always acted on them; usually by taking or sending round some home baking or a bunch of flowers. But inner promptings should not be equated with 'a word from the Lord', with all the seriousness that that implies.

If inner impressions and special revelations are to be treated with caution, there is no doubt that resort to astrology and other kinds of 'psychic' guidance is absolutely forbidden. God said to the Israelites, when they stood on the border of the Promised Land, speaking through Moses: 'When you enter the land the Lord your God is giving you, do not learn to imitate the detestable ways of the nations there. Let no-one be found among you ... who practises divination or sorcery, interprets omens, engages in witchcraft, or casts spells, or who is a medium or spiritist or who consults the dead. Anyone who does these things is detestable to the Lord.'[24] One of the evidences of a turning to the Lord by the Ephesians, following Paul's preaching, was that 'A number who had practised sorcery brought their scrolls together and burned them publicly.'[25]

2. *What about the use of a 'fleece' or 'casting lots'?*
Gideon, in the period of the Judges of Israel, sought assurance of God's guidance by asking for a miraculous sign. He put out a wool fleece, and asked God that he would confirm his proposed action by making the fleece wet when all the ground around was dry; and it was so. Then, to make absolutely sure, he asked that the next night the reverse might happen; the fleece be dry and the ground around wet with dew. Again, it was so.[26] Gideon went ahead with confidence, and God granted him success.

Many perplexed Christians have followed Gideon's example – with varying results. Should this action be recommended? On the whole, I think not. Gideon, though a chosen servant of God, had no Bible, and very little experience of God's ways at that stage in his life.

Then, what about 'casting lots'? It was certainly used in Biblical times; even occasionally in the early church. After the death of Judas, when the apostles felt the need to appoint a successor, they employed this method – after prayer that God would use it to resolve their dilemma.[27] Their action is not criticized, directly or indirectly. Neither Christ, nor his apostles in their letters, comment on the procedure. John Wesley resorted to the casting of lots at some crucial points in his ministry, but few mature Christians have followed his example in this regard.

3. *What about feelings and peace of mind?*
Many people consider that a sense of peace about a decision is confirmation that it was a right one, and that a lack of such a sense points to the need for further thought and prayer. The verse that is sometimes quoted in this context: 'Let the peace of Christ guide all your decisions'[28] is probably irrelevant to this debate, because it seems to refer to the matter of living at peace with others.

Whilst feelings cannot be ignored, they cannot be regarded as a safe guide to being in the will of God. Feelings are influenced by a variety of bodily and emotional states; such as illness, stress, insomnia, being in love, and also by our personality, e.g. whether we are sanguine or melancholics. Feelings can also be influenced by conscience – whether sensitive or insensitive. I know a professing Christian who left his wife to marry another man's wife. He argued: 'It is right because it feels right.' Peace of mind may simply reflect the fact that we have got what *we* want.

The great thing is to walk in obedience, and trust God about the feelings. The prophet Isaiah put it like this: 'Who among you fears the Lord and obeys the word of his servant? Let him who walks in the dark, who has no light, trust in the name of the Lord and rely on his God.'[29]

**Walk in obedience, and trust
God about the feelings**

---

4. *How do I recognize a missionary call?*
Every Christian, whatever his or her position, should be a missionary in the sense of being an ambassador for Christ in a world which does not recognize his rule. Jesus said to his disciples in his Sermon on the Mount: 'You are the light of the world.'[30] (For more about this, see chapter 12.) Nevertheless, there is a sense in which there is a special call to some of Christ's disciples to serve him outside their country and culture of origin. Every child of God should seriously consider whether this avenue of service may be God's will for them. How do we decide if it is? This is a big subject, and there are many books dealing with it. A recent and very readable one is Michael Griffiths' *Tinker, Tailor, Missionary?*[31]

Some basic considerations are the question of having a gift of speaking to others about Christ and in explaining the gospel to them. This is important, but it is probably even more important that others should recognize your gift; particularly the leaders of your local church. You may have a personal sense of 'call'; but if it is truly from God, it will almost always be recognized in due time by spiritually minded leaders. If you feel that God is calling you to specific missionary service, at home or abroad, I would suggest asking for an opportunity of praying with your church leader or elder about the matter.

5. *Have I missed the way?*

When things do not seem to be working out as we had hoped, there is a temptation to think we have missed the way. I have certainly had this experience. When I repeatedly failed to get the consultant appointment which was the next logical step in my career, and for which I was well trained, I began to wonder if I had been deaf to God's call to overseas service. I do not think that was the case, and it subsequently became clear that God had more to teach me in a junior position before I was ready for the more important job he had for me.

When we have made a decision along the line of God's will, it is natural to think that subsequent events should confirm the rightness of the course we have taken. We expect to sail into calm waters. But that is not necessarily so. Often it is the opposite. One has only to think of the disciples of Jesus in the storm on the lake of Galilee. They had set out at Christ's clear command.[32] He ordered them to go. Yet they encountered such a storm that they were afraid they were going to be drowned. Clearly, subsequent events do not necessarily prove the rightness or wrongness of a decision.

The safety net

Of course, being human, we do sometimes make wrong decisions. Even if we do so, I believe God is able to bring good out of the situation eventually. Edith Schaeffer, in her book *A Way of Seeing*, tells the story of a girl who came to stay at her home, L'Abri, in Switzerland. Jane was helping to prepare food for the week-end. Mrs. Schaeffer gave her favourite recipe for a sponge cake, to make whilst she did other jobs. After a time, Jane came to show her a strange yellow, sticky, gluey mixture, saying: 'Is this what it is supposed to look like? Shall I put it in the pan now?' 'Oh no,' said Mrs. Schaeffer, in a horrified tone. 'Please don't; it is not right at all. You've left something out, I'm sure.' 'No, I'm sure I haven't. I followed your instructions exactly.' 'You *must* have forgotten something,' repeated Mrs. Schaeffer. After checking and re-checking, Jane remembered that she had left out the sugar! 'Shall I throw the mess out and start

54

again?' Jane asked. 'No, wait; we can't afford that,' Mrs. Schaeffer said, putting her hands protectively over the bowl. 'Egg, salt, baking powder, flour, water – What can I do with that? Wait while I think.' Then she had an inspiration: noodles! Mrs. Schaeffer proceeded to add more flour; mixing, kneading, rolling, until it was paper thin. Then she cut it into little strips to make lovely noodles; not for dessert, but for soup: perhaps not so attractive, but certainly not wasted.[33]

The apostle Paul's statement, 'In all things God works for the good of those who love him'[34], is true even if we make mistakes. As a student, I was 'cocky', and incurred the displeasure of the most powerful professor in the medical school. I believe this effectively blocked the possibility of my anticipated return to Bristol. If so, I am sure that it worked for good, even though it caused considerable disappointment for many years. I am convinced that God over-ruled my mistake to bring about his own purpose.

References
1. Psalm 25:9
2. Proverbs 3:6
3. James 1:5
4. Hebrews 13:5, 6
5. Clifford Longley, *The Times,* 15th February 1992.
6. 1 Corinthians 7:28
7. 1 Corinthians 7:21

8. 1 Corinthians 10:24-31

9. Psalm 32:8, 9

10. Philippians 1:9, 10

11. Garry Friesen, *Decision Making and the Will of God*, Multnomah Press, 1980, p 277.

12. Psalm 66:18 (AV)

13. Ezekiel 3:5

14. Proverbs 12:15

15. Proverbs 15:22

16. Isaiah 64:4

17. Charles Stanley, *The Wonderful Spirit-filled Life* 1992, p 207.

18. Acts 16:9

19. Acts 19:21

20. Acts 20:3

21. Titus 3:12

22. 2 Corinthians 1:15-17

23. Romans 15: 24

24. Deuteronomy 18:9-12

25. Acts 19:19

26. Judges 6:36-40

27. Acts 1:23-26

28. Colossians 3:15 (J B Phillips)

29. Isaiah 50:10

30. Matthew 5:14

31. Michael Griffiths, *Tinker, Tailor, Missionary?*, IVP, 1992.

32. Matthew 14:22

33. Edith Schaeffer, *A Way of Seeing*, Hodder and Stoughton, 1977, p 77.

34. Romans 8:28

Chapter 4

KEEPING THE GOAL IN SIGHT

Some years ago, a reporter from one of the English daily newspapers set out to discover the secret of success by interviewing men who had reached the apex of their business or profession. One of them summed up the situation in these words: 'I think you will find with all the people you interview in this project – indeed, I think you will find this with most people who are successful – that they all have two main things in common. The first is that they know what they want. The second is that they have the energy to carry it through. If you never take "No" for an answer, nothing is impossible.'

After orientating oneself to a true view of success, there comes the task of working it out in practice. Once we have determined to take a Christian and not a materialistic view of success, we can learn a great deal from our worldly-wise colleagues, misdirected though their energies may be. So let us consider for a moment these two ingredients of success: a clear objective and determination.

A clear objective

First, there must be a clear objective. Remember Admiral Mahan's maxim: 'When you are trying to accomplish something, you should first decide what is the *final object* you are seeking to attain – and then never lose sight of it.' There is a Russian proverb to the effect that if you run after two hares, you won't catch one.

At any given time, there are near and distant objectives. Both must be defined. In the early years, the near objective is often an examination, which must be passed; and this must be kept clearly in view. But, even at this stage, it is good from time to time to take the long view. Of course, the ultimate objective may have to be re-defined if the immediate objective is not attained. If you cannot gain admission to a veterinary school or a nursing college, you have to revise your ambition of becoming a vet or a nurse. But it is always good to have an ultimate objective, even if it is provisional. If you limit yourself to short-term goals, you are likely to look back on a zig-zag course, without much progress.

In defining the ultimate objective, it is advisable to try to see what is going to be important in the future; to watch for new and promising developments. It is also vital to 'think big'. The research student, for example, should consider some of the great unsolved problems in his or her field of study, and ask what will matter most in ten or twenty years time. It is important not to be a sheep – not to follow the crowd. It is helpful to consider the variety of openings in one's business or profession in relation to one's particular aptitude. For example, in my own profession of medicine, there are openings in administration, research and teaching as well as in general practice and hospital medicine. It is good to consider the less popular specialities, because advancement is likely to be quicker in them. These used to include psychiatry, anaesthetics, radiology and community medicine; but fashions change, depending on advances in understanding of disease, new diagnostic methods and new forms of treatment. I coached a student in the year behind me for his final examination, and he became a consultant in radiology ten years before I attained a similar status in general medicine – a speciality for which there was considerably greater competition. He was happy in his speciality, as I was in mine.

It is well worth considering work overseas, especially if one has an aptitude for learning languages. There are many countries, both in Europe and further afield, where there are great opportunities for Christian witness based on business or professional work. Overseas experience expands the horizons and introduces new and valuable ideas. As Robert Frost put it:

Two roads diverged in a wood, and I –
I took the one less travelled by,
And that has made all the difference.[1]

Determination

First, then, it is essential to have a clear objective
and never to lose sight of it. The other prerequisite
for success is determination. Remember the
words of the successful businessman: 'They know
what they want ... and they have the energy to
carry it through.' There is no short cut; hard work
and persistence are essential. David Livingstone
started life as a child factory worker in a cotton
mill. But he was resolved that his life should count
for God. He had few advantages, but he had
determination, and he realised that he had to help
himself. He had no time to study during the day,
so he did it at night. By strenuous efforts, he
qualified himself by the age of twenty-three to
undertake a college curriculum.

Talent is developed by challenge and
competition. It has often been said that
Mendelssohn never achieved the greatness which
his talents deserved, because success came to him
too early. That may or may not be true in
Mendelssohn's case, but there is no denying that
the difficulties which come to most of us are
necessary for developing our characters. Winston
Churchill's daughter, Lady Soames, said in a TV
broadcast, that without the 'wilderness years', her

father would not have been able to lead Britain in her darkest hour, when she stood alone against the might of Germany and Italy. Determination must be combined with flexibility. Circumstances may make it impossible to attain the goal directly. Success demands adaptability.

Discipline

One of the main ingredients in determination is discipline. The apostle Paul was fond of likening the Christian life to a race, with its need of discipline. He said: 'Like an athlete, I punish my body, treating it roughly, training it to do what it should, not what it wants to.'[2]

Everyone who desires to achieve success needs to discipline his life; to put first things first. It is easy to waste time. I am not suggesting that there should be no breaks from work. On the contrary, periods of recreation are essential; and I have no doubt that the day of rest was ordained by God for our good. (I deal with the use of time in chapter 6.) It is the wasted minutes that need to be captured and put to good use; the purposeless chats over endless cups of coffee. As Gordon MacDonald has put it: 'We need to seal the "time leaks".'[3] William Barclay cites the English poet Samuel Taylor Coleridge as a tragic example of indiscipline. He was enormously gifted. In his head and in his mind, he had all kinds of books, but he would not face the discipline of sitting down to write them out. Barclay concludes: 'Never did so great a mind produce so little.'[4]

Failure to achieve can often be traced to lack of discipline. There are a hundred and one diversions and snares for the unwary; but there are three whose effect is particularly far-reaching and disastrous. The first of these is in the realm of sexual indulgence. The pressures here can be enormously strong and subtle, and there is need for constant vigilance; because the results of indiscipline are devastating. It is not without reason that God forbids sexual intercourse outside marriage and also homosexual practices.

> **Everyone who wants to achieve success needs to discipline his life; to put first things first**

Homosexual orientation is not blameworthy. Indeed, I regard it as a disability which calls for sympathy and understanding. Homosexual practice, on the other hand is condemned in the Scriptures of both the Old and New Testaments.[5] Encouragingly, Paul indicates that the Corinthians had changed their life-style since they became Christians.[6] Homosexual practice must be resisted in the same way that fornication and adultery must be resisted by those with powerful heterosexual inclination.

There are many case histories to show that

sexual immorality is one of the greatest saboteurs of the discipline and determination needed for success. The story of Samson in the book of Judges is a case in point. He failed to achieve lasting success commensurate with his outstanding strength because of his philandering and lack of commitment to his vocation. Up to date examples among politicians and others in high places are, alas, not difficult to find. The Book of Proverbs gives a number of brilliant pictures of the attractions which are laid out to tempt the foolish and which end with what the author vividly likens to 'a bird darting into a snare, little knowing that it will cost him his life.'[7]

The two other great snares are alcohol and drugs; and it is essential to exercise the utmost care with both. (I have more to say about this in chapter 10).

Factors outside our control

Endowment
It is important to attempt to make a realistic evaluation of our talents. Although it is unpopular to recognise it in today's egalitarian climate of opinion, it is sheer blindness to overlook the fact that there is great inequality of gifts between one individual and another. In this sense, at least, all men are not equal. Some have a brilliant intellect. Others have a phenomenal memory. Others again

have a strong constitution and are able to do with very little sleep. In one of Jesus' parables, he spoke of one man being given five talents, another two and another one.[8] Most of us have only one or two talents, and we are wise to recognise our limitations.

It is no use aiming too high, because this only leads to intolerable stress and eventual breakdown. On the other hand it is no use aiming too low, because this leads to boredom and frustration. It is a great help to regard success not in terms of our attainment in relation to others, but as the fulfilment of our God-given potential. Fortunately, it is not always the fastest who wins the race of life. Often the tortoise overtakes the hare. One talent developed can do more good than five neglected or misused. Many of those to whom the world is most indebted have had one talent which they used to the full. Think, for example, of the patience and scrupulous attention to detail of those who compiled biblical concordances in the days before computers became available to complete the task in one thousandth of the time; or of Peter Mark Roget, for that matter: what would writers do without him?

Chance
Another factor outside our control is that of chance. What would generally be called 'luck'

played a crucial role at several points in my career. My endowments are not exceptional, but I have been exceptionally fortunate. In a crucial scholarship examination, I was given a difficult experiment in physics; but it was one which I happened to have done before. This enabled me to go to Cambridge University, which would otherwise have been out of the question.

There is the luck of being in the right place for a vacancy at the right time. This was true in my case. When I came back from the Second World War, I was looking for a post as a trainee (registrar) at the same time as a cardiologist happened to be looking for an assistant. This was the start of a career in cardiology. The most amazing stroke of 'luck' came in my early days as a consultant in Aberdeen, as I have already described. The fact is that a great deal depends on opportunity, both in upbringing and education, and in the fortunate circumstances which enable a person to demonstrate and develop his or her talents.

Samuel Johnson, compiler, in 1755, of the landmark Dictionary of the English language, wrote an essay *The Uncertainty of Life*. In it, he emphasized the part played by chance. He said that if a person reviews the way in which he has reached his present position, he will find that every event in his life has been, as he put it, 'influenced by causes acting without his intervention.'[9] Napoleon recognised the importance of chance in military affairs, and it is said that one of his main requirements for his marshals was that they should be lucky!

Where does 'luck' come from? Dr. Johnson accepted the Christian view that God is in control of all events. In the essay already referred to, he went on to say: 'In spite of appearances, God is in control of all events. Nothing in reality is governed by chance, but the universe is under the perpetual superintendence of him who created it.' I fully agree with this concept, and I see all the good things that have happened in my own life as the undeserved blessing of God.

> **God is in control of all events. Nothing in reality is governed by chance**

If we have this conviction that God is in control of all events and that his providential care surrounds us, we need not fret when things appear to go wrong, or pull strings in order to achieve our own ends. All success comes ultimately from God.

It has often been observed how important discoveries have occurred seemingly by chance. The discovery of penicillin is a familiar example. The word serendipity has been applied to this phenomenon. Having said this, it is equally true that chance favours the prepared mind, just as fortune favours the brave. When a successful

golfer was accused of just being lucky, he replied:
'The funny thing is that the more I practice, the
luckier I get.'

References
1. Robert Frost, 'The Road not Taken', from *The Poetry of Robert Frost* (Cape 1972) p.105.
2. 1 Corinthians 9:27 (Living Bible)
3. Gordon MacDonald, *Ordering Your Private World* Highland Books, 1987, p.80.
4. William Barclay, *The Gospel of Matthew*, Westminster, 1975, p.280.
5. Romans 1:18, 21-2, 26-7; 1 Corinthians 6:9, 10
6. 1 Corinthians 6:11
7. Proverbs 7:23
8. Matthew 25:14-30
9. Samuel Johnson, 'The uncertainty of life', in *Samuel Johnson: selected writings*, ed. R.T. Davies, Faber and Faber, 1965, p.26.

Chapter 5

PRIORITIES AND AMBITIONS

Once having become convinced of the true nature of success, and having identified some sort of objective, it is necessary to keep this in our sights, to work it out in practice and maintain right priorities in everyday life.

A personal history

Early in student life, I became impressed with the words of the Lord Jesus Christ in the Sermon on the Mount: 'Seek ye first the kingdom of God, and his righteousness: and all these things shall be added unto you.'[1] (It was the Authorised Version in those days.) One of my brothers describes how he found this text inscribed on the fly-leaf of my Pathology test-book! Later, when I graduated to being a junior doctor, I conceived the idea of making out what I called Priority Cards, which I kept constantly before me and revised every two or three weeks. At the top of each card I put my motto: 'Seek first the kingdom of God'. Then I set out my priorities for the period ahead. On one side of the card, I listed my work objectives, and on the other side, I noted my spiritual objectives.

My work involved keeping up to date with

medical advances, lecturing, writing and research. So on one side of the card I listed in order of importance the reading and preparation which I planned to cover in this area. On the other side, I listed such duties as what part of the Bible to study, what books to read, what lesson or address to prepare, and further possibilities in this sphere. Of course, a list is of no value unless it leads to action. It must be consulted frequently and acted on. I kept mine in the wallet in the pocket of my jacket, where I was often reminded of it.

When, eventually, I obtained an established appointment, I took a longer perspective and set down my objectives for the foreseeable future. The plan ran as follows:

Overall aim (as before) – to 'seek first the kingdom of God and his righteousness'.

Method:

1. Seek to glorify God by doing the work for which I was paid to the best of my ability.

2. Witness for Christ among patients, staff and students.

3. Strengthen the Christian witness in my local church.

4. Strengthen the Christian witness in the locality.

(By 'witness', I meant trying to live as a Christian and being ready to give a reason for my Christian belief.)

Living as a Christian

Some committed Christians might question the order of importance given above; particularly putting work before witness: but I have no doubt that this is the right way round. A surgeon who had served as a missionary in the Far East used to say: 'Christian opportunity depends on medical efficiency.' This dictum was based on his overseas experience, but it is equally true at home, and in all forms of secular work. The apostle Paul wrote to the Christians in the Turkish city of Colossae: 'Obey your earthly masters in everything; and do it not only when their eye is on you and to win their favour, but with sincerity of heart and reverence for the Lord. Whatever you do, work at it with all your heart, as working for the Lord, not for men, since you know that you will receive an inheritance from the Lord as a reward. It is the Lord Christ you are serving.'[2]

Whatever profession or business we are in, and even as students, we are constantly under the scrutiny of our colleagues; and this is doubly so if we claim to be Christians. No amount of talking can make up for shoddy work. So our priority should be to do our work, whatever it is, to the glory of God. Indeed, we should endeavour to make every part of life, our work as well as our specifically spiritual activities, an offering to God. Charles Simeon, the chaplain to King's College, Cambridge, in the nineteenth century, used to impress upon his students that 'the plain duties of the hour and day, however secular on their surface, were sacred things.'

This matter of putting God first in our daily work is so important and so often forgotten that I make no apology for emphasizing it. Soon after I commenced work in Aberdeen, I came across some words attributed to Francois Mauriac which deeply impressed me. 'As for me, I must say once again that I am a Christian, first and last; which means a man who feels himself responsible to

> **The plain duties of the hour and day, however secular on their surface, are sacred things**

God and to his conscience for the epoch that he lives in. I am a man who feels that, however inadequate he may be, he has been put here to play a certain role among his fellow men and for his fellow men. He is engaged; it is not a question of deliberately engaging himself.'

This is surely true of each Christian. I felt it was true of me as I entered on my new post: 'Responsible to God ... however inadequate ... put here to play a certain role.' It seems to me that this is particularly relevant to those periods of our lives when we do not seem to be getting anywhere. God has put us there 'to play a certain role'. There is a great temptation to think we cannot really begin our life's work for God until we are settled in some definitive post, where we will have some control over our time and environment. The truth is that in some cases, the most fruitful work is done as a student, or as a trainee. Sometimes it has turned out that there has been no other similar opportunity later in life.

At a wedding reception recently, I found myself sitting next to an old man whom I had not met before, about whom I knew nothing, and who was almost stone deaf. I could see that any conversation was going to be difficult, and would be overheard by a wide circle of guests. I had the bright idea of asking him what he looked back on as the most exciting period of his life. I did not need to ask another question. He told me that as a young man, he was involved in the Second World War, and was taken prisoner early on. He was a committed Christian, and wanted to do something for God. He found there were no church services for the prisoners, so he asked a chaplain for permission to organize a weekly hymn singing. Only four came the first time, but the numbers rapidly built up to well over one hundred and continued for many months. Throughout his life, he had retained his zeal for God, but he had never again found a comparable opportunity for serving him.

'Called' or 'Driven'

Gordon MacDonald draws an instructive contrast between what he terms 'called' people and 'driven' people.[3] 'Called' people are those who see their work as a vocation – a call from God. 'Driven' people, on the other hand, are those whose aim is to make something of themselves. MacDonald lists some of their characteristics:

*They tend to be gratified only by accomplishment;

* they are pre-occupied with the symbols of accomplishment;

* they tend to be caught up in the uncontrolled pursuit of expansion;

* they have a limited regard for integrity. In the attempt to push ahead relentlessly, they lie to themselves about motives. Values and morals are compromised.

* They have limited or undeveloped people skills;

* they are highly competitive;

* they often possess a 'volcanic' force of anger; and

* they are abnormally busy; usually too busy for the pursuit of ordinary relationships in marriage, family, or friendship, too busy even to carry on a relationship with themselves – not to speak of one with God. They tend to experience 'the barrenness of a busy life', and end up in 'burn-out' (see chapter 11).

Ambition

Some people regard 'ambition' as a dirty word. But it is not wrong for a Christian to be ambitious. Our Lord was ambitious. He expressed his aim as being 'to do the will of him who sent me and to finish his work.'[4] The apostle Paul was ambitious. He said: 'Forgetting what is behind and straining towards what is ahead, I press on towards the goal to win the prize for which God has called me heavenwards in Christ Jesus.'[5] Whether ambition is right or wrong depends on what the goal is and whether it is really worth going for. The two tests I would apply are these. First, would the attainment of your ambition really satisfy you? Would it make you happy, and if so, for how long? Secondly, is your ambition worthy of a Christian? How will it look in the light of eternity?

Many young men hope to make a lot of money, to drive a fast car, to excel in sport, to get to the top in their job. Some young women have similar objectives. Others hope to get a nice home of their own, to wear 'designer' clothes, to be able to entertain lavishly, to marry a handsome man and to have a marvellous family. There is nothing inherently sinful in such ambitions, provided they are kept subservient to the will of God. The question is: Do such achievements bring satisfaction? And for how long? Everyone knows that money doesn't bring lasting happiness. The pursuit of fame or position brings constant trouble from rivals. If you do find the perfect boy or girl, we all know that youthful good looks don't last. Happy families inevitably break up when the children leave home. The common reaction to retirement is the realisation that achievements are over and, looking back, so little seems to have been done.

> The world and its desires pass away, but the man who does the will of God lives forever

But retirement is not the end. There may be many years of life left – and there is still the judgment seat of Christ. The apostle Paul paints a vivid picture of this as an occasion when our deeds will be 'tested by fire'.[6] If we have built with 'gold, silver and precious stones' the work will stand. If we have built with 'wood, hay, stubble' it will all go up in smoke. It is the clearest possible warning to go for the things that last; to build for eternity. The apostle John puts it like this: 'The world and its desires pass away, but the man who does the will of God lives forever.'[7]

Paul had the gifts and talents that would have enabled him to make a name for himself in anything he turned his hand to, but he set all that aside, counting it as 'mere garbage', as he graphically described it, in order that he might know Christ, become like him, and fulfil his will in his life.[8] He rejected earthly, temporary rewards for the 'crown that will last for ever', which God gives to those who love him.[9]

So is ambition wrong for a Christian? No; not if it is rightly focused. Jeremiah said to his secretary Baruch: 'Are you seeking great things for yourself? Don't do it.'[10] That looks at first sight like a prohibition against ambition. But note the words 'for yourself'. It is selfish ambition which is wrong. But ambition like Jeremiah's and Paul's – to do God's will – is right. It is really simply a matter of logic and common sense. Do you want to achieve something that outlasts time? Of course you do. Do you want to respond appropriately to the amazing love of God in sending his own Son to die on the cross to make it possible for you to share his heaven? Of course you do if you stop to think about it. Indeed, you might be prepared to say with Isaac Watts:

Were the whole realm of nature mine,
That were an offering far too small;
Love so amazing, so divine,
Demands my soul, my life, my all.[11]

77

Some ambitious Christians convince themselves that their worldly success automatically brings glory to God and is a testimony to the outside world that Christianity works. It may do so, if it is accompanied by humility and an acknowledgment of God as the source. There are undoubtedly many examples of committed Christians whom God has blessed and prospered in various fields of endeavour and has used to his glory. But there are many more whose names are virtually unknown who have had an enormous influence in extending the kingdom of God.

> **There is frequently a conflict between ambition and integrity**

Advancement may be an advantage to Christian service when the believer is determined to maintain spiritual priorities. It may provide increased scope for serving the Lord both in business or profession and also in the church. A high income level also makes strong stewardship possible. On the other hand, some Christians, in aiming higher than their abilities allow, have become so over-stressed and over-stretched that their work has entirely consumed them.

The Rev. Peter Masters, pastor of the London Metropolitan Tabernacle, sets out five tests we can apply to ourselves to determine whether our aims are valid:

* If the love of substance, status or possessions has become the driving force and motivating factor in our lives, our aims are covetous.

* If these things are seen as the key to happiness; the only way to gain uplift; the only source of relief, and the only answer to our problems, then our aims are covetous.

* If the pursuit of status and things is at the expense of Christian service, once again, our aims are covetous.

* If advancement is sought for self-exaltation and esteem, our aims are certainly covetous.

* If the desire for earthly gain has secured a grip on the heart, so that we always need something else, or something more, then our aims are covetous.[12]

It is interesting to note the difference in the way ambition is understood in North America compared with Britain. In Britain, ambition tends to be an uncomplimentary word. To describe someone as ambitious often implies that he or she is self-seeking, dominating and ruthless. In American terms, on the other hand, to have ambition is to be highly motivated. The traditional question asked about any prospective suitor by a girl's father is: 'Does he have any ambition?' The opposite of having ambition is being a bum (a waster)![13]

There is frequently a conflict between ambition and integrity. Ambition often brings with it a temptation to compromise. In business circles, there may be a powerful inducement to go along with dishonest practices. In academic circles, there may be pressure to conceal differences of opinion in order to keep in with the head of the department. In theological circles, there may be a temptation to compromise integrity in our principles; e.g. to appear to accept a 'liberal' interpretation of Scripture against our better judgment. Selfish ambition inevitably leads to moral corruption. As James says in his epistle: 'Where you have envy and selfish ambition, there you find disorder and every evil practice.'[14]

Dietrich Bonhoeffer faced this problem as a theological student in Germany in the 1930s, when Hitler was bent on dominating the church. Bonhoeffer was ambitious. He wanted his life to count for the kingdom of God. He wanted to be remembered after his death as having made a significant contribution. He could have gained a high position in the church by compromising his beliefs, but he renounced the lure of short-term success in the name of fidelity to Jesus Christ. Bonhoeffer stands as an example of God's Word: 'Those who honour me I will honour, but those who despise me will be disdained.'[15] Bonhoeffer's name is highly respected and honoured, whilst those of his colleagues who compromised are regarded with contempt. In totalitarian regimes, the call to integrity poses dreadful problems. Russian Christians who were unwilling to accept Communism lost their jobs. German pastors who opposed Hitler lost their lives.

In contrast to ambition, indeed almost the opposite, is what Americans call 'downshifting' and 'voluntary simplification'. This is a reaction to the phrenetic rush and madness of so much of life in 'the fast lane'. It represents a decisive choice in favour of a way of life in which work and home are more balanced. Most of those who have adopted this course have been forced into it by redundancy and an inability to return to full-time employment; but some have chosen it voluntarily. The aggressive city life which determines that a man leaves home at 6.30 am and doesn't return until 7 or 8 pm in the evening can destroy family life as effectively as infidelity. Furthermore, such single-minded dedication to achievement and career inevitably communicates itself to the children who feel under intolerable pressure to achieve similarly.

Distinguishing the urgent from the important

If we are to maintain right priorities, it is essential to learn to distinguish the urgent from the important. This was memorably pointed out by Dr. Charles Hummel in words which find an echo in my experience. He wrote:

> Our lives leave a trail of unfinished tasks; unanswered letters, unvisited friends, unwritten articles and unread books. We find ourselves working more and enjoying it less. But it isn't hard work that hurts us, but doubt and indecision which produce anxiety.... The greatest danger is letting the *urgent* things crowd out the *important*.... The problem is that the *important* thing rarely has to be done today, or even this week.... The *urgent* tasks are the ones that call for instant action. They seem at the moment to be important and irresistible, so they devour our energy.... If the Christian is too busy to stop, take a spiritual inventory and receive his assignments from God, he becomes a slave to the tyranny of the urgent. He may work day and night to achieve much that seems important to himself and others, but he will not finish the work God has for him to do.'[16]

How true this is. We are all in danger of letting the *urgent* things crowd out the *important*. As a result, the important things never get done. We need to be prepared to cut our losses and jettison projects which we come to see are not going to be valuable in the long run, just as we throw away things that clutter up the home or office.

We must beware of 'short-termism'. There is a strong temptation to give preference to projects which will come to fruition quickly and attract immediate notice, rather than those which will not yield results for several years. A similar tendency is seen in Christian work. Have you noticed that when a series of Bible studies is being planned, it is the short books which are preferred: Timothy, Titus, James and the epistles of John rather than Romans, Corinthians or the Gospels.

In this chapter, I have been trying to set out the Christian's priorities – but I have missed

---

**Our greatest danger is letting the
urgent things crowd out the important**

---

something out. Have you noticed the omission? Where does the spouse and family come in the scheme of things? Don't they have some degree of priority? Of course they do. I deal with that in the next chapter.

References
1. Matthew 6:33 (AV)
2. Colossians 3:22-4
3. Gordon MacDonald, *Ordering Your Private World* Highland Books,, 1987, p.35.
4. John 4:34
5. Philippians 3:13-14
6. 1 Corinthians 3:13-15
7. 1 John 2:17

8. Philippians 3:8 (TEV)
9. 1 Corinthians 9:25; 2 Timothy 4:8
10. Jeremiah 45:5
11. Isaac Watts, *When I survey the wondrous cross*
12. Peter Masters, 'Is it wrong to seek advancement?'*Sword and Trowel*, Metropolitan Tabernacle, 1995, issue 1, p.24.
13. Janet Daley in *The Times*, 21st April, 1995.
14. James 3:16
15. 1 Samuel 2:30
16. Charles E. Hummel, *Tyranny of the Urgent*, IVCF of the USA, 1967.

Chapter 6

THE ALLOCATION OF TIME

One of the greatest problems for the Christian business or professional worker who wants to make a success of life is the pressure of time. Its right allocation is one of the secrets of success.

Time is, of course, a problem for most people in responsible jobs, whether Christian or not. But it is probably true to say that, in general, Christians are under even greater pressure than their non-Christian colleagues. In addition to their regular commitments, which they must discharge to a high standard for the glory of God, they feel a responsibility to make time so as to be available to meet the personal and spiritual needs of their colleagues and clients; if such help is sought and welcomed. They also have the responsibility of playing an active part in their church. All these extra, yet vital, commitments take up a great deal of time. The result is that many committed Christians in business or the professions are stretched to a point of inefficiency, and need to cut down in order to concentrate on the most important things.

The big question is: What are the most important things? A useful basic rule, attributed to Dr. H. Clay Trumbull, is: 'Do first the things you are paid to do, then the things you have promised to do, then the things you would like to do.' Let us examine each of these categories in turn.

The things you are paid to do

If we are in receipt of a salary, our primary commitment is clearly to our employer. We must fulfil our contract both in the letter and in the spirit. I know a Christian doctor who, finding himself under increasing pressure on account of extra commitments, undertook a time and motion study to satisfy himself that he was doing the sessions he was contracted to do.

If our work-load is too heavy we must take decisive steps to cut it down, being prepared to accept a cut in salary, if necessary. When I was serving with the Royal Army Medical Corps in India during the 1939-45 War, a lance-corporal with whom I served refused promotion because he felt he could serve God better in a lowly rank. I also know of a number of professional people who have cut their work-load (and their pay) in order to spend more time in direct Christian work and with their family. Our primary commitment is to do the work we are paid to do, and do it to the glory of God. It is a matter of simple honesty and integrity.

The things you have promised to do

This may mean different things to different people. We all tend to make promises to do jobs for our friends or colleagues without thinking through the implications. Then, when we find that they conflict with our interests, we are tempted to renege on them. This is wrong. The Psalmist describes the godly man as one who 'keeps his oath, even when it hurts'.[1]

'The things you have promised to do.' It seems to me that if we are married, our most important duty under this heading is to our wife or husband. This is a commitment we have entered into voluntarily and explicitly. It is something we have promised to do. Divorce is a breach of that promise. Most Christians stay together for the sake of the family, but there are few sadder sights than that of a middle-aged couple, worn out with the pursuit of worldly success, who have not made time to enjoy each other's company or that of their children, drifting apart to spend their closing days in loneliness; or continuing to live together as strangers in declining health, when all conjugal and family love and tenderness have vanished. Sir David Llewellyn MP gave sound advice when he said, in an open letter to a new MP: 'No matter what success you will have achieved, if your progress has been bought at the price of family, children, friends – or conscience – it will turn to dust and ashes in your mouth.'

Since, according to Christ's teaching, man and wife are 'one flesh'[2], they should search jointly for the will of God for their lives. It is not a question of sacrificing career to marriage and family, or vice versa, but a sincere joint search for the will of God for them as a couple – by praying together, and by talking and listening to different points of view. If husbands and wives are to find time for each other, it is essential to look ahead and earmark dates in the diary for this purpose. Otherwise, as I know only too well, it usually happens that when the one is free, the other is not. If the couple is blessed with children, it is important to note in advance the dates of key events at school and college.

I have to confess that there have been periods in my life when I took my wife too much for granted and neglected my responsibility to our family. If my wife had not been so resourceful and understanding and forgiving, this neglect might easily have led to disaster. I still retain several touching letters she wrote to me at times when I was away at conferences or on lecture tours, urging me to make more time for her and for the children when I returned. I resolved to do so – though with limited success. We sometimes got a baby-sitter and went out together for a meal, and I sometimes told the children stories at bedtime. But my contribution was meagre, and it is only by the mercy of God that our marriage is still strong after nearly fifty years and all the children are committed to serving God in one way or another.

Rob Parsons in his valuable book *Sixty Minute Father* makes the same point. He confesses that he still finds it difficult to forgive himself for the occasion when he had no time to watch his son play baseball. In his commendation at the front of the book, Sir John Harvey-Jones states his view that being a good father is the most important success of all.[3] James Boswell, the biographer of the great Dr. Johnson, looked back on the day his father took him fishing as the highlight of his

---

**Do first the things you are paid to do,
then the things you have promised to do,
then the things you would like to do**

---

childhood. When his father's diary came into his hands, he looked to see if he had any entry for that day. He had, and it read: 'Went fishing with James – a day wasted'!

Much of a parent's influence is unconscious. My father gave me relatively little direct instruction, but the example of his life was powerful. One particular car journey with him left an indelible impression. When he noticed the milometer move up to the figure 10,000, he pulled off the road, took off his hat, and gave thanks to God for another ten thousand miles of his protection. It taught me a lesson of dependence on God and acknowledgment of his goodness far more effectively than any words could have done.

A strong marriage is an enormous strength to a worker who is under pressure. Conversely, a fragile marriage is a source of constant weakness. This duty is, of course, lighter if there are no children, or none at home, and heavier if there are several young children or children at a 'difficult' age.

The things you would like to do

Only when we are doing the things we are paid to do and the things we have promised to do are we in a position to take on additional commitments. Into this category come the various extras of life. These may be connected with our business or profession; such as research, writing, examining and consultancy work. They may be social or political, or they may be spiritual activities of one kind or another; or they may be hobbies. The whole area of additional commitment is a vitally important one, because it is here that the really difficult decisions must be made. To my mind, there is no problem about the things we are paid to do and the things we have promised to do. These are clear duties. For most family men and women at some periods of their lives, these duties may amount to a full life, and allow no time for additional commitments at all; but for most, there is some leeway. (I consider this question further in chapter 11, on Avoiding Burn-out.)

Gordon MacDonald points out that time must be budgeted in the same way that we budget money. Unallocated time tends to be used inefficiently in things we are not good at and which should be devolved to others. Time which is unallocated can easily come under the influence of dominant people who try to dictate how we use it – against our better judgment. Furthermore, unallocated time tends to be taken up inappropriately with emergencies – the old problem of the urgent crowding out the important. There is also a strong temptation for it to get invested in things that gain public acclaim or the approval of our peers rather than in things which are more important in the long run.[4]

> **Time must be budgeted in the same
> way that we budget money**

Rhythms of maximum effectiveness

There is a wide variation between one individual and another in regard to the time of the day when they are able to work most effectively, and it is important to take this into account in planning the best time to undertake creative work. Some are 'larks'; they wake with the light and are brightest in the morning. Others are 'owls'; they function best later in the day, and can often work on long into the night.

Individuals vary too in the amount of sleep they need. Most need seven to nine hours, but some need as much as ten hours if they are to work effectively. A few, on the other hand, can manage on six hours or less. Such people obviously are at an advantage in having additional time for work. It is no use trying to manage on too few hours of sleep, because the time saved will not be used efficiently. The amount of time needed for sleep falls with increasing age; though in the elderly, this is balanced to some extent by a nap after lunch.

Obviously, creative work, and work that demands close concentration, should be done during that part of the day during which we find we are at our brightest. It is valuable to have another task to switch to when the first one is not going well and one feels bogged down.

Late nights are a problem for 'larks'. Evening engagements pall, and interfere with mental alertness the following day. If one has a routine of rising early, it is sometimes possible to excuse oneself with the apology: 'I've an early start tomorrow.' Those who make a habit of starting the day with God could truthfully say: 'I have an early appointment tomorrow!'

Redeeming the time

Dr. Stephen Adei, a Ghanaian who rose from humble beginnings to become a United Nations diplomat, has some valuable advice about 'redeeming the time' based on his own experience. 'The first principle of effective time management,' he says, 'is the ability to redeem some otherwise wasted time each day, and to apply that consistently to self-improvement and the achievement of certain well-targeted goals.' That requires discipline, because there are only twenty-four hours in each day, and the greater part of these is predetermined for certain functions. Sleep, work and travel, meals and other essentials leave only about two hours free. But, as Stephen Adei says: 'The good news is that two hours is all you need to succeed.' The first principle of effective time management is to capture those two hours and to dedicate them to good and effective use.[5]

The problem is that in this modern age, there are certain things that tend to eat up time, especially watching TV. One thing about TV is that even though you often put it on specifically to watch one particular programme, it is only too easy to leave it on for the next and the next and the next. It is essential to be disciplined to redeem the time. Many students fritter away time in endless coffee-table discussions. Dr. John White, the Christian psychiatrist, makes the point that many Christian committee meetings are badly planned and consume an unnecessary amount of time. He suggests that it may sometimes be right to walk out of such a meeting with: 'Please, Mr. Chairman, I have to leave now.' Then get up and go. If the chairman protests, smile and say: 'I'm sorry, but you'll have to manage without me.'[6]

Redeeming the two or so hours, and making quality use of them, is vital to time management. Stephen Adei has a specific recommendation for students: 'Try to redeem those two hours, if possible, early in the morning. For example, if your classes start at 8 am and you require one hour to eat, dress and get to where you are supposed to be, then your two hours must be redeemed between 5 and 7 am.' He says: 'Some people have the habit of going about everything the wrong way. Instead of going to bed at 10 pm, they watch films, good and bad, till the early hours of the morning. They then wake up tired and limp.... The most wasted hours of the day are from 6pm to midnight – a solid six hours, which is a quarter of the whole day. Wise use of those hours will be like expanding your life by 25%. Redeem part of it, and since you may be tired, use part to add to your hours of sleep, if you can't study.... Remember that you *can* change your routine. Human beings can adapt to new routines in twenty-one days if they mean to.'

Of course, we are all made differently, and

what suits one may not suit another. Nevertheless, such advice, based on experience and wide observation of others who have made a real success of life, must be taken seriously.

Periods of relaxation

It is important to build some period of relaxation, however brief, into each day. It sounds impossible to do this on busy days, but such breaks have a rejuvenating effect and make the rest of the day more efficient. Indeed, it may be better to have a shorter period of sleep and budget for the balance to be used for one or more periods of relaxation during the day.

Two hours is all you need to succeed

The Christian can rest in the knowledge that God 'knows how we are formed'.[7] He knows our need for periods of relaxation. We can also rest in the sovereignty of God, and the knowledge that if we rest in him he will undertake for us. The Rev. William Still of Aberdeen, who exercised an immense influence through his preaching and writing until well into his eighties, described how he made a habit of lying on a bed, fully stretched out, for ten minutes or so. He recommended consciously relaxing every muscle in the body, starting from the head and moving progressively down to the feet.[8] Another aid to relaxation which he recommended is conscious focusing on one's breathing. For many people, relaxing in a reclining position is better than lying in bed. A nap of 10-20 minutes is often enough to provide refreshment of mind for the remainder of the day.

Leisure and recreation
Some form of leisure activity is essential to health and success. For most of human history, life has made greater physical demands upon people than it does today. The majority worked with their hands, and domestic chores alone involved a level of labour which would appal us today. In the past, the human frame endured a heavy physical workload, whereas nowadays the only parts of

---

Some form of leisure activity is essential to health and success

---

the body to be regularly exercised are the fingers! At home, knobs and switches shield us from most of the old chores. Obviously, there is a case for some compensatory exercise. The Rev. Peter Masters defines Christian leisure as 'the science of counteracting the unnatural physical under-use of the body, and also of counteracting the overstrain produced by the nervous and emotional pressures of modern life.'[9]

Many find recreation in sports of various kinds. Walking can be not only a relaxation, but also an aid to creative thinking. '*Solvitur ambulando*' said the ancients, speaking of a difficult problem. 'It is solved by walking.' There is a double truth here. Problems are often solved as we just go steadily on. Also, it frequently happens that the solution is found on a walk, either in solitude or in the company of a good listener.

For the Christian, exercise in the form of walking can have an added dimension in the enjoyment of the natural world. For him, the observation of the created world, and the appreciation of its sights and sounds, is the exploration of the works of God 'who richly provides us with everything for our enjoyment.'[10] So recreational activities can have a spiritual as well as a physical and mental benefit. Most sports engender discipline and in addition provide interaction with other human beings, both Christian and non-Christian.

Reading is valuable, both as a form of recreation and for its effect in broadening the mind. This is true of history, biography and the works of the great novelists. Some find relaxation in studying specialized subjects like geology or photography. Those whose work involves a considerable amount of reading to keep abreast of their speciality may not have much appetite or time for recreational reading; especially if they are involved in preparation for teaching a Bible

Class or adult group. For much of my professional life, I found myself in this situation and had to make do with reading the book reviews in the newspaper and noting two or three to take on holiday.

The great danger for many people is not the failure to recognize the importance of leisure, but the tendency to want too much of it. For some, there is a real danger of leisure activities becoming an 'idol'. Richard Baxter who exercised an influential ministry in Kidderminster, England, three hundred years ago, set out some principles to bear in mind in evaluating the appropriateness of leisure activities. He would ask: 'Do they take precedence over our duty to God? Do they take up too much time? Are they too costly? Do they involve covetousness or tend to stir up covetousness in others? Do they involve cruelty to other people or to animals? Do they indulge thoughts that are inappropriate for a Christian?' The ultimate purpose of leisure activity is to keep the body and mind fit for the service of God. As the apostle Paul puts it: 'Whatever you do, do it all for the glory of God.'[11]

Time for God

Christians down the ages have felt the need to 'fence off' a part of the day, in order to be able to focus their minds on God in prayer and meditation on his Word, the Bible. I am convinced that this is a good habit. Admittedly, it is often difficult to find time at the beginning of the day. This is particularly so at certain periods of life when sleep is disturbed by irregular working hours or by the demands of small children. I know, because I have experienced nights interrupted by the call of duty, and my wife had prolonged periods of disruption when each of our five children was small. But we have rarely found it impossible to start a day without committing ourselves specifically into God's hands, however briefly.

Many people have told me that at some periods of life they have found the evening to be the best time for this exercise. I would simply make two points. The first is that if it is postponed until evening, it may be lost altogether on account of interruptions of one sort or another, or clouded by tiredness. If an exercise is really important, it needs to be given top priority. The second point is that one objective of the exercise is as a preparation for the day ahead. It is an opportunity to ask for God's help and also to carry a part of his Word in our mind, as we go about our duties. There is little point in tuning the instrument after the concert. Having said that, the important thing is to have quality time rather than prescribed time. It is important to add that there should be no feeling of guilt if occasionally there is no time to do more than pray: 'Into your hands I commit my spirit.'[12]

The use of Sunday

Another question that arises for the Christian in the allocation of time is the use of Sunday. For some, there are duties which restrict freedom of choice; but for most of us, most of our lives, we are free to determine how we spend the day.

A century ago, the rules were clear and definite. The command: 'Remember the Sabbath day by keeping it holy'[13] meant, for the British Christian at least, that the first day of the week was to be kept set apart for God; not only positively in church attendance and spiritual

> **We need a day when we can turn our thoughts specifically to eternal things**

exercises, but also negatively, in the avoidance of all labour that was not strictly necessary. This meant the avoidance of games. The story of the athlete, Eric Liddell, who refused to run a crucial world championship race on a Sunday, is well known thanks to the film *Chariots of Fire*. For many, it also meant the avoidance of travel, shopping and newspapers.

More recently, there has been a change in Christian thinking. It is now emphasized that our Lord criticized the religious leaders of his day for their absurd rules regarding Sabbath observance. Moreover, the apostles did not appear to stress the keeping of the Sabbath. Nevertheless, it cannot be denied that the fourth commandment is embedded in the Decalogue, and that none of the other nine commands has been abrogated. So, it is probably best to accept that the fourth command is relevant today, as in the past, but that it has to be kept in the spirit rather than in the letter. In my view, we 'keep the Sabbath day holy' when we do acts of mercy and kindness to others, and engage in activities which enhance our service for God.

I would say without hesitation that Sunday is best kept different and special. In past generations, Sunday was prized as a day of physical and mental relaxation. Even if we do not work such long hours as they did, we still need a day when we can turn our thoughts specifically to eternal things. As Wordsworth wrote: 'The world is too much with us. Late and soon, getting and spending, we lay waste our powers.' We need to pause and contemplate God and eternity. In the entrance to King's College Chapel, Aberdeen, there is a plaque with a quotation from John Bunyan. It reads: 'Here one may, without much molestation, be thinking what he is, whence he came, what he has done and to what the King has called him.'

In my view, there is no need for the rigid dos and don'ts which were taught in the past. This was Christ's criticism of the religious leaders of his day. Nevertheless, the general principle of a day when we can think about God, read his Word, and be encouraged by meeting with other Christians, is immensely valuable. It is good for us as individuals, and it is good for the family. During my War service in India, I was struck by the fact that each Army vehicle had a label on its windscreen bearing the initials MD, followed by an abbreviated name of one of the days of the week, e.g. 'MD Thurs'. This indicated that one day in each week was a maintenance day when the vehicle was off the road.

The Sabbath can be regarded as part of the total attitude of resting in God. Just as we rest in God for our salvation, so we rest in him for the provision of all our needs. I think this is the lesson God was teaching the Israelites in the wilderness, when he did not provide manna on the Sabbath. He wanted them to realize that if they obeyed his commands, they could depend on him to meet their needs.

Even when the pressure is on, with examinations looming, Sunday can still be kept special. I never opened a work book on a Sunday; not because I was bright enough not to need to do so, but because I felt that if I made good use of the other days, I could safely commit the outcome to God.

It takes many people a long time to realize that rest and peace in our hearts makes us not only more healthy, but also more efficient. It is a case of '*recueillir pour mieux sauter*'; 'pause, in order to advance'. Recreation and a right use of Sunday keep us fresh physically, mentally and spiritually.

Sometimes, success depends on being ready in emergency. Have you ever thought of the number of times in the Bible record when men were called by God for specific service, without warning, on one occasion only? If they had not been in a fit state of mind, they would have missed out on their greatest opportunity. Think of Ananias whom God sent to act as obstetrician in the new birth of Saul of Tarsus, soon to become Paul the apostle. Ananias was plodding along, presumably doing a good job in Damascus. Then suddenly God called him to go to an address in Straight Street, where there was the work of a lifetime.[14] If he had missed that, because he was too tired or out of fellowship with God, no one would ever have heard of him; but now millions know the name of Ananias of Damascus. The same thing happened to a score of people in sacred history. Prophets appear out of the blue, do a crucial job for God, once and once only. Similar things happen today; so we need to be ready. Spending time regularly with God is essential to readiness.

References

1. Psalm 15:4
2. Matthew 19:5
3. Rob Parsons, *The Sixty Minute Father* Hodder and Stoughton, 1955
4. Gordon MacDonald, *Ordering Your Private World* Highland Books, 1987, pp.73-86
5. Stephen Adei, *Keys to Abundant Living with No Regrets,* Capital Press, pp.57-60.
6. John White, *The Fight* Inter-Varsity Press 1977, p.213.
7. Psalm 103:14
8. William Still, *Rhythms of Rest and Work,* Gilcomston South Church, Aberdeen, 1985, pp.25-28.
9. Peter Masters, 'The Christian's rules for leisure activities and possessions' *Sword and Trowel,* Metropolitan Tabernacle, 1994, issue 3, p.6.
10. 1 Timothy 6:17
11. 1 Corinthians 10:31
12. Psalm 31:5
13. Exodus 20:8
14. Acts 9:10-17

Chapter 7

AIDS TO EFFICIENCY

Good organisation is essential for efficient work. In the previous chapter, I emphasized the importance of organizing one's time schedule to maximize efficiency. In this chapter, I deal with other ways in which efficiency can be increased.

A personal filing system

Everyone should have a well-arranged personal filing system, and this cannot be started too early. The details vary according to one's interests, but the principle is to plan four main sections: two related to work – one general and the other specialized – and two others. In my case, the two related to work were general medical and my speciality; cardiology. The two non-professional sections were domestic and spiritual.

Within each section, there are a number of individual files. In the general medical section, I have files in which I preserve articles or notes on alcoholism, the alimentary system, blood diseases, and so on, in alphabetical order. In the special interest section, I have files on coronary disease, disorders of heart rhythm and so on.

In the domestic section, I have files for bank, car, current correspondence, home non-electrical, home electrical, and so on. In the spiritual section, I have files covering local church affairs, Christian organisations I am interested in, as well as files for the different sections of Scripture: Pentateuch, historical books, Psalms, etc., and doctrines, such as Christ, the Holy Spirit, prayer, etc.

In each section it is important to have a miscellaneous file for items which do not fall readily into any specific file. When any subject in the miscellaneous file grows to a sufficient size, the relevant material can be transplanted into a file of its own. I have also found it useful to include a 'think' file for ideas which I want to come back to and develop when I have more time.

Much of the filing can now be handled by computer in a way which was not possible when I started; but the principle remains the same. For some time to come, much of our information is likely to come to us in the form of newspaper articles, periodicals, photocopies and faxes. So files where papers can be stored will still be needed.

Other aids to efficiency
The appropriateness of other aids to efficiency depends on the nature of one's work and the money available. The simplest and least expensive is a notebook; yet how valuable it is for recording fleeting ideas and important duties.

Darwin used to keep a notebook for recording observations out of keeping with his ideas, lest he should forget them.

When I do not have a pen and notebook readily available, I have found a small electric recorder invaluable for saving ideas which come to mind. I use it when walking or driving, or when relaxing in a reclining chair, and I have it beside my bed at night. I have a poor memory, so when a potentially important idea comes into my mind, it is necessary for me to record it immediately. Once this is done, it frees my mind to roam over other ideas. I have used such a machine for thirty years, and would have no hesitation in rating it the most valuable gadget in my possession.

For those who have to do a lot of telephoning in circumstances in which a secretary is not available, an attachment which amplifies the signal is a great boon. This allows the caller to go on working at his desk with both hands free while waiting for the person to whom he wants to speak to answer the phone. It is important to learn to type, even inexpertly, and to master the use of a word processor.

High specialisation tends to sterility. For anyone concerned with research or teaching, it is essential to maintain a wide range of interests, because valuable ideas may be drawn from unexpected fields. I have found it useful to read a quality newspaper in order to see statements in print. Often, I only have time to read the urgent items on the actual day. Other articles of interest, I tear out to read later at leisure. Another piece of advice is to keep several tasks running in parallel, so that when fatigued at one, it is possible to switch to another. The most intellectually exacting tasks can be done at the time of day when one is brightest, and the less demanding ones at other times.

If our work is dull and routine, and every job has an element of this, it is stimulating to try to become an expert in some aspect of it. I found that my work involved doing a large number of home visits, most of which involved recording a standard electrocardiogram, and giving an opinion as to whether an attack of chest pain was due to coronary heart disease. Nothing much had been written on this subject so I decided that I might as well specialize in it. It formed the basis of several research papers. I have heard of someone who became an authority on some aspect of office work. People used to say: 'Phone up the office and ask to speak to so-and-so.' It didn't lead to immediate promotion, but it gave an added dimension to her working life.

Chapter 8

APPLYING FOR JOBS

In today's world, uncertainty about the future looms large. What jobs are available? What would be best? These questions have always exercised students and senior school pupils. Now they re-surface intermittently throughout life.

When applying for a job, it is natural to want to advance one's career by all the means available. Up to a point this is right and necessary. But in all our applications, we need to think and act as Christians, and to remember that our future is secure in God's hands. We need to realise that God has a plan for our lives and that he is well able to bring this about without any string-pulling on our part. God's promise is clear and definite: 'In all your ways acknowledge him, and he will make your paths straight.'[1] This rules out any dishonesty or underhand ways on our part.

Before deciding what job to apply for, it is wise to seek advice from several mature and experienced people. Sometimes this creates problems. The 'boss' may offer specific advice about what post to apply for. In this case, even if the suggestion is made casually, it is important to realise what you are doing if you do not follow it. Honesty and openness are important. If you decide to follow a different course of action, try to explain to your adviser why you are doing so.

The written application

It is wise, at an early stage in one's career, to seek the advice of an experienced friend about the best way of setting out one's application. In Britain, though not in all countries, it is the rule that they should be typed. The presentation should be neat but not ostentatious. The key points should be obvious, and excessive detail should be avoided. It is a tradition in Scotland that applications are not judged on their length but on their 'weight': i.e. their importance.

It is important to make one's curriculum vitae (CV) relevant to the particular post being sought. If possible, the CV should be kept on floppy disc so that it can be customised for each job application. It should be printed out using a good printer, so that it will photocopy well.

Most CVs are rather dry and factual. Dr. Philip Wellsby has suggested that they could be made more attractive by adding sections headed 'Review of career to date' and 'Future career intentions'.[2] These are not essential, though they do give the applicant the opportunity of portraying himself or herself as a person rather than the owner of a list of attributes. This background is invaluable for interviewers, because it assists them in framing penetrating and informative questions which the applicant should be prepared to answer. It is important to 'sell' oneself. If you have an interesting hobby, mention it; and if you are a non-smoker, say so.

If the CV contains gaps or entries that appear disadvantageous, the 'Review of career' section can be used to pre-empt critical questions by making these disadvantages appear beneficial. For example, 'The period of unemployment enabled me to do things which I was not able to do whilst I was busy working.' These should be specified, giving concrete examples.

The covering letter which accompanies the CV is important. It is often the first thing the shortlisting official sees. Unless your handwriting is particularly attractive, the letter should be typed. Give your name, address and telephone number, and say where you saw the advert. The letter should be short and include a statement along the lines: 'I am particularly interested is this post because ...'. Say what you are looking for, and end: 'I look forward to hearing from you.'

Since many applicants for a post have broadly similar qualifications, the aim must be to make your application stand out. One aid to this is to attach an attractive passport size photograph of yourself to the top sheet of the CV. It is important to make sure that both the photograph and the CV can be copied satisfactorily, because shortlisters and interviewers do not see the originals.

Referees should not be taken for granted. Permission to use their names should always be courteously requested. If applications are infrequent, the referees should be informed that you have applied for a specific job. Always send a copy of your job application to your referees. If you are repeatedly unsuccessful in your applications, your referee should then take more interest and give you appropriate advice – especially if your account of your career to date contains favourable mention of your time with him or her.

A good CV will get you an interview, but it will not get you a job. That depends on the impression you make at interview.

The interview
Dress in a way which is appropriate to the job you are seeking. Go, prepared for a long wait; with an empty bladder! At the interview, don't wave your hands about. If possible keep them underneath the table. Think carefully before answering questions which involve expressions of opinion. Appear relaxed, even if you do not feel it. At the end of an interview, the candidate is usually asked: 'Have you any questions you would like to ask us?' This requires care, because you should have discovered the answer to all

important questions before the interview. In general, it is best to reply: 'No. All my questions were answered when I visited the firm (or hospital, etc.).'

Other comments

It is often better to go for a poorly paid post in a good firm or department where there is a prospect of promotion, rather than a higher paid job in a poor establishment, which may prove to be a dead end. This is, of course, a difficult decision if there are heavy financial responsibilities.

Timing is as important in professional life as in cricket. A batsman may hit a ball hard, but if he strikes too soon or too late it will not travel far, and he may jar his hand into the bargain. On the other hand, if he strikes at the correct time the ball will speed comfortably towards the boundary. Academic and professional people often cause themselves much stress and disappointment by trying to get things too soon; for example by pressing for admission to membership or fellowship of a professional association too early. The Christian can afford to be patient and await God's time.

What about those who have suffered numerous rebuffs in their attempts to secure a steady job or an established appointment, and who consider they are marking time and their talents are being wasted? I have every sympathy with those in this position. I myself went through two or three months of unemployment at an early stage in my career, and had many years of waiting and a score of applications before I secured my ultimate appointment. I deal with the subject of disappointments and difficulties in the next chapter, so at this point I will simply give it as my testimony that God is faithful and dependable, and his word is true: 'God ... acts on behalf of those who wait for him.'[3]

References
1. Proverbs 3:6
2. Philip Wellsby, 'Interview View', *Proceedings of the Royal College of Physicians*, October 1989, p. 499.
3. Isaiah 64:4

Chapter 9

DELAYS, DISAPPOINTMENTS AND DIFFICULTIES

Problems and difficulties lie across the path of every human being; and the Christian is by no means exempt. They often arise suddenly, 'out of the blue', and seem to be utterly undesirable hindrances, not only to the achievement of our hopes and aspirations, but also to the task which we believe God has given us to do. For the trainee there may be the failure to obtain a diploma for which you had worked hard, or an appointment for which you were well qualified and which would have led on to the goal upon which your heart was set. It is sometimes difficult to understand these disappointments, and they may lead us to question what had previously been regarded as certainties. We may be tempted to doubt God's guidance and his love.

The problem of waiting
The most difficult period of my life was the period as an experienced 'junior' doctor in London. I was a senior registrar, fully trained for a hospital specialist appointment, but unsuccessful in obtaining one. The waiting period was long; ten

years, in fact. It seemed endless. I felt deeply discouraged. I doubted my abilities, and wondered whether I would ever get a worthwhile job. Above all, it raised the question whether I was where God wanted me to be or not. Should I be overseas – my wife and I had often thought and prayed about this – or should I be aiming for general practice rather than for a hospital appointment?

At the time, it is certainly difficult to see these periods of delay and uncertainty as blessings. They seem the utter reverse. And yet one knows from first principles that they must be so, and that as the apostle Paul put it: 'In *all* things God works for the good of those who love him.'[1] It is immensely reassuring to realize that God is constantly at work in our life. Often – though not always – one can later see that what seemed to be a disaster was indeed a blessing in disguise.

During the period of waiting, I ran into a serious disagreement with my boss, who was also my main backer. We had worked together on an important research project and were within sight of publication. He insisted on including some material which appeared to me to be unscientific, and which I could not accept; and he seemed totally impervious to my argument. If he could not be dissuaded, I would have to withdraw my name from the publication. This would have damaged our relationship and left me with nothing to show for two years work, at a time when I desperately needed to make progress. I prayed earnestly for guidance and for God's over-ruling in the situation. Then God came up with an amazing answer. My boss asked the professor of the department in which the work had been done, to add her name to the publication. He knew she would be flattered by the invitation, but he was certain she would refuse, because she had not made any contribution to the paper. To his surprise, she accepted – and insisted on excluding the contentious material! Truly 'God moves in a mysterious way, his wonders to perform.' This experience made me realize that God has surprises up his sleeve!

The support of Christian friends

In times of frustration and disappointment, one is thrown back on one's resources. I was fortunate in that I had a grounding from childhood in the knowledge of the infinite power and wisdom and love of God. I was also fortunate in having the friendship of experienced Christians, and particularly the love and devotion of a wife who was in the fullest sense a partner – sharing the same basic truths and ideals.

After years of waiting, when nothing was in sight, my wife and I received, out of the blue, a letter from a Christian leader which had a profound effect on us both. Indeed, we have often had occasion to refer back to it. It ran as follows:

'My dear Joan and David,

Here are a few lines which, through the years, have often been a great help to me, and I pass them on to you with love, and a prayer that you may find them helpful too:

'The main end in life is not to do, but to become. For this we are being moulded every hour. You cannot understand why, year after year, the stern ordeal is perpetuated; you think the time is wasted, you are doing nothing. Yes – but you are situated in the set of circumstances that give you the best opportunity of manifesting, and therefore acquiring, qualities in which your character is naturally deficient. And the Refiner sits patiently beside the crucible intent on the process, tempering the heat and eager that the scum should pass off and his own face become perfectly reflected in the surface.'

He went on:

'Forgive me if I seem to be preaching a sermon! But I once passed through an experience lasting a number of years, which I thought at the time would really break and crush my spirit. Looking back on that dark valley I see now that in it, and out of it, came some of the most important and valued lessons of life which I would not have missed. I am sure it will be so for you both, so hold on, till the light breaks, for it will.'

I have quoted this letter at length, because it is a reminder of three things. In the first place, it expresses clearly one of the most important purposes behind God's use of delays and disappointments and 'bad times': namely, the development of character – like the refining of a valuable metal. We need constantly to be reminded that 'The main end in life is not to do but to become.'

In my case, my besetting sin was, undoubtedly, pride. My repeated failure to get a consultant job hit that firmly on the head. I was brought to realize that anything I achieved was God's goodness rather my doing. The apostle Paul says that suffering produces character.[2] The apostle James goes so far as to say that we should actually rejoice and count ourselves fortunate when we are faced with trials.[3] Experience of adversity and failure can be immensely valuable if we realise that God is in control, and don't give way to despair.

The main end in life is not to do, but to become

The letter I quoted above also shows how a discouraging experience equips the sufferer to help others: 'I once passed through an experience ....' I have, over the years, often found myself able to encourage others on the basis of my experience. I recently came across the copy of a letter I wrote to a member of my medical team after he had failed to get a consultant post for which he had justifiable hopes. I ended my letter with these words: 'I see you will be forty this month. I was over forty-one when I got my consultant appointment. I did, however, have the advantage of knowing that God was in control and that he had just the right place for me. This was my sheet anchor.'

Thirdly, it illustrates the value of a letter of encouragement, sent at the appropriate time under the guidance of the Holy Spirit, to someone who is suffering acute disappointment. Such letters are not easy to write. They cannot be 'dashed off' or easily dictated to a secretary. We must be able to say, as Pope John XXIII said of his diary: 'My soul is in these pages.' They need not be long. From the same hand that penned the letter quoted above, I received some years later the following terse note: '... tells me you have arthritis to a handicapping extent. I am so sorry. May God give you courage to *accept* it – *adapt* yourself to it – and *adorn* it.'

Why God allows frustration and delay

Looking back, I can see my long period of waiting as a profoundly important epoch in my life. It was valuable for allowing completion of a research project that would have been impossible in a more responsible and busier appointment. It was valuable on account of the close links that I forged with many leaders, both in my profession and in Christian life. It was valuable too for the experience it gave in helping to found a church in a new housing area. But no doubt its greatest value was in the development of character. It taught me a lesson which I have never forgotten;

namely, that success is in God's hands.

Delays and disappointments often raise the question: Am I in the line of God's will, or have I turned aside? Have I taken a wrong turning somewhere? Have I missed God's guidance? If I am in the right path, why has God allowed this? If only I had acted differently at some point, this would never have happened. Such questioning is futile. God has promised to guide his children. 'Who, then, is the man that fears the Lord? He will instruct him in the way chosen for him.'[4] 'He guides the humble in what is right, and teaches them his way.'[5] It is a general principle in the Christian life that if we are willing to do God's will, he will lead us in his way as we wait upon him. In times of doubt we need to fall back on our knowledge of God. He is infinitely wise – too wise to make a mistake. He is infinitely powerful – too powerful to be thwarted in his purpose. He is infinitely loving – too loving to give us needless pain; but also too loving to leave us as Peter Pans when we might grow to full manhood. C. S. Lewis put it well when he said that if we plead to be spared chastening, we are asking for less love and not more.[6]

The value of hymns
In times of difficulty, my wife and I have often found help from hymns. A favourite has been John Wesley's translation of Paulus Gerhardt's

Befiehl du deine Wege. In some English hymnbooks this commences: 'Put thou thy trust in God ...'; in others: 'Commit thou all thy ways ...' We have found the following verses particularly helpful:

Through waves, and clouds, and storms
He gently clears thy way;
Wait thou his time; so shall this night
Soon end in joyous day.

Leave to his sovereign sway
To choose and to command;
So shalt thou wondering own his sway,
How wise, how strong his hand.

Far, far above thy thought
His counsel shall appear,
When fully he the work hath wrought
That caused thy needless fear.

Frustration in later life

Adversity may be encountered at any period of life. Loss of privilege and status in middle and later life is particularly hard to bear. This is becoming a common experience now that jobs are far less secure. Even when there is no immediate threat to our job, frustration is a common problem. It is encountered in Christian work as well as in our business or profession. It may arise either from opposition or administrative inertia. Edmund Burke, the famous British politician of the eighteenth century, said: 'Those who would carry on great public schemes must be proof against the most fatiguing delays, the most mortifying disappointments, the most shocking insults, and worst of all the presumptuous judgments of the ignorant upon their designs.' It is then that we need the gifts for which Reinhold Niebuhr prayed: 'Serenity to accept what cannot be changed; courage to change what should be changed; and wisdom to distinguish the one from the other.'

Nothing matters when one comes to the last hour but a clear conscience before God

---

Adversity is a test of integrity. When one is under pressure, there is a temptation to cut corners, to bend the rules, and stifle one's conscience. It is in these circumstances that one is tempted to be dishonest in money matters, such as submitting false claims for travelling allowances. I often think of the words of Edith Cavell, who was head of the Red Cross hospital in Brussels during the First World War, and was imprisoned and executed by the Germans. Whilst awaiting death, she wrote: 'The thought that you have done before God and yourself your whole duty, and with good heart, will be your greatest support in the hard moments of life and in the face of death. Nothing matters when one comes to this last hour but a clear conscience before God.'

Unemployment

Periods of unemployment are the experience of millions today, and the threat of unemployment hangs over millions more. It is a fact of modern life and we have to live with it. Short periods without work and pay, and the threat of it are a cause of great anxiety. Long periods are deeply demoralizing. I had only a brief experience of such a situation, but I can still recall the sense of hopelessness and failure which it bred. I can remember standing on the edge of a railway platform, and thinking how easy it would be to fall forward, apparently accidentally, as the train was approaching.

Those who have not experienced unemployment might think that a great deal could be achieved by wise use of the leisure provided. Some have, indeed, used the free time to do more in the home and release their spouse to take a part-time, or even a full-time, paid job. Others have helped the church by undertaking cleaning or visiting, or helping house-bound members with their shopping or gardening. Others have used the time to study the Bible or to pray more. But in practice, it seems that relatively few have been able to make constructive use of it. Periods of illness have been used for reading and the cultivation of new interests. I had a great deal of leisure in the Army, and managed to master the elements of New Testament Greek. But illness and leisure do not sear the soul in the way that unemployment does.

The responsibility of caring for young children seriously interferes with employment prospects. For gifted and ambitious women, it presents a major problem. As anyone who has done it knows, it is actually busier than most paid jobs. My wife trained as a doctor, but was only able to practice for a year or two before our first child arrived. She was not free to return to professional work for seventeen years. The physical and emotional demands of bringing up a family can be deeply frustrating to a career woman. Fortunately, my wife took the view that being a whole-time home-maker is the most important work that anyone can do. She did it willingly – and successfully. Sometimes the task falls to the father rather than the mother. In either case, it must be regarded as a work of immense strategic importance; one on which the stability of the family – and indeed the nation – largely depends.

References
1. Romans 8:28
2. Romans 5:3, 4
3. James 1:2
4. Psalm 25:12
5. Psalm 25:9
6. C. S. Lewis, *The Problem of Pain*, The Centenary Press, 1940, p.31.

Chapter 10

PITFALLS

Each stage of life has its own peculiar dangers.
Some strike early, and cease to be a problem later.
Others only surface powerfully in middle age.
To be forewarned is to be forearmed.

College and early career

It is necessary to post a warning notice at the start
of each new phase of life. It applies equally to
the first fortnight at college and the first days of
a new job. It faced me in my first days in the
Army. The point is this. It is important to take a
stand as a Christian right from Day One. A
university lecturer, who spent a lifetime teaching
and observing students, put the warning starkly:
'If during that period he does not show his
colours, avoids those who are trying to keep the
flag flying, and chooses his friends among
unbelievers, experience shows that, as a rule (to
which, thank God, there are exceptions), his
spiritual life receives a wound from which it never
recovers.'[1]

Another danger period is a time of extra busyness and fatigue. During such a period, the quiet time with God may be curtailed or one may be too tired for it to be spiritually refreshing. There is also a temptation to seek comfort where one can find it, which may well be from a non-Christian of the opposite sex. This may lead to a close friendship, and a turning of the heart away from God. We cannot overlook the fact that the Christian is engaged in a life-long battle against the world, the flesh and the Devil; and that the Devil is the master of subtle temptation.

> **It is important to take a stand as a Christian right from Day One**

Later life

In my work as a doctor, and especially in private practice, I was impressed with the discovery that so many of the patients who came to consult me on account of exhaustion – most of them business or professional people – had nothing physically or psychologically wrong with them, but were simply tired out by the 'rat race'. They had come to feel that, for them, there was no alternative to longer and longer hours of work and greater and greater intensity of effort. To call a halt to the advance would be to slip rapidly backwards. The time to take a break and really enjoy living was always round the next corner. They seemed to me to be the perfect illustration of Jesus' parable of the rich farmer who had had a bumper harvest and now had no barns large enough to store his crops. The only solution he could see was to pull down his barns and build larger ones. Once this was done, he was convinced he would be able to take his ease, 'eat, drink and be merry'. But this time never came, because he suddenly died.[2]

The strain inherent in so many jobs, and the pressure to take on increasingly heavy commitments so that life is dominated by work, is a common cause of breakdown. Yet these pressures by themselves are rarely the sole explanation. Lord Moran, Winston Churchill's doctor, wrote: 'I doubt whether men at the top often go to bits through overwork itself. There are generally other less obvious factors dragging them down.'[3] What are the 'other less obvious factors'? In my experience as a doctor, overwork commonly leads to, or is accompanied by, neglect of physical, social and spiritual health. Let's look at each of these elements in turn.

Neglect of physical health

A common result of overwork is neglect of recreation. Every worker, and especially anyone who carries heavy responsibility, needs regular periods of rest and relaxation – and exercise. (I have dealt with this in chapter 6.) Physical needs vary greatly from one individual to another. Some can manage with very little sleep and short breaks; others need much longer periods of rest if they are to remain fully alert and creative. A wise old general practitioner colleague of mine, who grew up in a farming community, used to quote the adage: 'It is never a waste of time to stop to sharpen the scythe.'

Alcohol and drugs

A common reaction to overwork and the resultant tiredness is recourse to alcohol or drugs as a relaxant or stimulant. When the business or professional man comes home tired, he just wants to put his feet up and have a drink. Later, he starts

> **More careers have been ruined by alcohol than in any other way**

the habit of taking a drink at lunch time. So, by degrees, he starts on a progressive dependence on alcohol. It is probably true to say that more careers have been ruined by alcohol than in any other way. The seeds of the alcohol habit are often sown in student days. In many universities and colleges, heavy drinking is regarded as the normal way of celebrating the passing of an examination. The same applies to the celebration of success in sporting and other achievements.

Christianity is not a teetotal religion. Our Lord himself was known to take alcohol (in contrast with John the Baptist, who was a total abstainer). Jesus actually supplied a second round of drinks at a wedding party![4] There are, however, stern warnings in the Bible against intemperance. There is no doubt that if the use of alcohol is not carefully controlled, it becomes a terrible master. So it is advisable to view it with considerable caution. It may be best to abstain when in the company of those one does not know well, in case any of them has a dependency problem which they are trying to break.

The recreational use of other drugs is becoming increasingly common. Experimentation with cannabis, amphetamines, solvents and other agents begins in school and rises to a peak in the early twenties. Most of the drugs used are illegal, expensive, and have to be acquired from unreliable sources. This means that occasionally there will be a 'bad' product, which may prove fatal. There is also a tendency for the mildest and safest drugs to lead on to 'hard' drugs like heroin, which are very difficult to give up, and often have a ruinous effect on life. The warning which used to be given to those tempted to experiment with alcohol applies even more to drugs: 'Have courage, my boy, to say No.'

Neglect of family life
Another result of overwork is neglect of family life. The tired business or professional person

131

does not want to be troubled by the problems of the home and family. He (or she, because it applies equally to business or professional women) has enough of his own. He just wants to be left alone with the newspaper and the 'telly'. Some business and professional people regularly work late into the evening. What sort of family life do they have? How do they fulfil their duty to their spouses and children? We may not go to this extreme, but as I look at my colleagues, and indeed my own way of life, I have no doubt that many business and professional people do seriously neglect their spouses and families. As a result, husband and wife inevitably drift apart, and thus lose the vitally important stability of a calm and happy home life.

There was a moving report recently of an encounter between the Prince of Wales and a homeless pauper in London. The Prince did not recognise the middle-aged man who made his living by selling *The Big Issue*, until he said: 'Actually, we were at school together.' The pauper came from a privileged home, and went to the same school as the Prince. Afterwards, he did well for a time as a journalist and a writer, with a book which rose to number eight in the best-seller list. But while things were going well in his career, his private life was falling apart. Looking back, he said: 'I realised that I had not given enough time to my family and friends. I suppose the booze got me in the end. I lost my house, and one day I woke up in a shop doorway in the Strand. I had lost everything.'

There is no need to repeat what I have said earlier about the dangers involved in extra-marital relationships (See chapter 4). Many a promising public career has been ruined when adultery came to light. It is often argued that private misconduct should not be a disqualification for public life. But clandestine affairs *do* affect a person's efficiency, cast doubt on the reliability of their promises, and undermine their authority in dealing with subordinate staff. They also destroy the peace and support of a loving home. Everyone knows about the possibility of contracting AIDS, but even that is less serious than the devastating effect of infidelity on family life.

Neglect of spiritual health
Another hidden factor in breakdown is neglect of spiritual health. Few people are rank atheists. Most admit deep down to a belief in God, the creator and sustainer of the universe. Most would therefore agree, if they thought logically, that a life which has no time for the worship of God must be unbalanced and unhealthy. Nevertheless, there can be little doubt that private spiritual exercises and public worship are widely neglected. Those in the caring professions or teaching may salve their consciences by arguing

that their profession comprises their whole duty to God. A medical colleague of mine told me quite explicitly: 'My work is my religion.' Often the wife and children are left to attend church without the husband. It is important that whenever possible a Christian family worships together. There is a large element of truth in the saying: 'The family that prays together, stays together.'

Neglect of spiritual health leaves a fundamental weakness in the edifice of life. This explains the sudden ruin of many an apparently successful business or professional person. Many build a splendid superstructure, and give an admirable appearance to the outside world, but if there is no firm foundation, there is a great risk of everything collapsing. Gordon MacDonald likens this situation to the 'sinkhole' phenomenon. He describes how the residents of a Florida apartment block awoke to find that the ground beneath the street in front of their building had collapsed, engulfing the road and the cars on it, and threatening the building itself.[5] They did not realise that for years they had been living over a cavity.

The lure of money

Money can easily become an obsession and a snare, even to those who will happily sing 'Riches I heed not, nor man's empty praise'. I once saw, fixed to the back of the door of a university dean's office, a card with the words: 'Money isn't everything'. Below, in small print, it added: 'But it's a long way ahead of whatever is in second place'. I do not think money comes at the top of the list for many Christians. Nevertheless, it is extraordinary to see the lengths some will go to make a bit more. I have frequently been surprised at the way some of my busy colleagues, with a perfectly adequate income, take on additional work of a dull and routine nature simply to increase their earnings. Avarice often leads to dishonesty. This, in turn leads to a bad conscience and in some cases to a total loss of reputation.

> **Neglect of spiritual health leaves a fundamental weakness in the edifice of life**

An essay competition promoted by *The Times* newspaper jointly with the National Westminster Bank posed the question: 'Can a competitive business be ethical?' Business ethics is currently a hot subject. Scandals in business and political life have led to a greater public awareness and concern about standards of behaviour. Friends of mine in business have told me from their own first hand knowledge of false invoices submitted in order to claim extra Government support, and blatant bribery to get jobs done ahead of another firm. I know, in my own profession, of the temptation to claim expenses that were not incurred, and to divert funds donated for research into a personal account.

It can be especially difficult to act honestly when to do so will bring the dishonesty of someone else to notice. I was told of a nurse who did a regular clinic which never lasted more than half a session, but which she always claimed as a full session. A Christian did a locum at the clinic and naturally was not prepared to go along with this practice, to the fury of her colleague. In academic, as in business life, the ladder of promotion often involves a temptation to compromise.

If you love money, you can't love God; or as Jesus put it: 'You cannot serve both God and Money.'[6] Stephen Adei, the Ghanaian Christian whom I have already quoted, lays down some valuable advice on money management on the basis of his own experience. He came from a poor family, and says himself that he did not learn to manage his finances until middle life. Up to that time, he was continually in debt. Having learned the lesson himself, he passed it on to his children in the form of three principles: the first is to tithe, or give a tenth of one's income towards God's kingdom; the second to save and invest a further 10%; the third to live within 80% of income. Although these proportions may not be applicable to everyone, his advice that it is important to mark out the limits of one's basic needs and not allow one's lifestyle to be determined by one's peers, the Joneses, the media or family traditions, is certainly good. He sums up: 'Define your life goal and financial goals, write them down and stick to them.'[7] The Bible teaches clearly that wealth is in God's hands. 'The silver is mine and the gold is mine, declares the Lord Almighty.'[8] God is the one who gives us the power to make wealth.[9]

If you love money, you can't love God

Gambling

The introduction of a British national lottery has, predictably, increased significantly the number of individuals committed to gambling. It is argued in its favour that it raises money for the arts, music, sport and other good causes; and this is true. On the other hand, charities which are unwilling to accept money from gambling find that their support has declined.

Whatever arguments there may be for the lottery, I feel that from the point of view of personal discipline, the temptation to play it should be resisted. The fact that it is only the winners who receive publicity blinds the minds even of intelligent people to the logic of the situation; that statistically the great majority of gamblers are losers. In my view, gambling indicates not only a defect of the mind, but also of the heart; involving, as it does, a breach of the tenth commandment: 'You shall not covet.'[10]

References

1. A.R. Short, *The Rock Beneath*, Inter-Varsity Fellowship, 1955, p.10.
2. Luke 12:13-21
3. Charles Moran, *The Struggle for Survival*, 1966, p.99.
4. John 2:1-11
5. Gordon MacDonald, *Ordering Your Private World*, Highland Books, 1987, p.13.
6. Matthew 6:24
7. Stephen Adei, *Keys to Abundant Living With No Regrets*, Capital Press, p.78.
8. Haggai 2:8
9. Deuteronomy 8:18
10. Exodus 20:17

Chapter 11

AVOIDING BURN-OUT

School and college readers can skip this chapter

Many gifted and potentially successful people grind to a halt before they reach their goal. Most of those launching out into their first job have high expectations, both in terms of personal satisfaction and of doing something worthwhile. A fair number can look back later in life to periods when these expectations have been largely fulfilled. But all too many end up disillusioned, disappointed, having achieved relatively little, and having entered a state which has been colourfully described as 'burn-out'.

Burn-out is characterized by symptoms of tiredness, irritability, depression, violent temper outbursts, exaggerated emotional responses to small stresses, loss of freshness, vitality and *joie de vivre* ; often leading to mental exhaustion and a longing for early retirement. Frequently, there is loss of concentration and short-term memory, and loss of decision-making ability, leading to low productivity and a deterioration in standards. There is also a sense of lack of fulfilment and disappointment, tinged with bitterness over what is seen as an absence of due recognition.[1] Such a state carries with it the temptation to resort to excessive amounts of alcohol and drugs. Furthermore, it is often disastrous for the marriage and for family life. The spiritual life inevitably suffers too.

Causes of burn-out

Why do so many business and professional people, including Christians, get into this state? If we could identify the causes, it should be possible to avoid the outcome. One of the factors is, undoubtedly, prolonged physical, and especially mental, overload. It is a phenomenon reminiscent of the physiological principle called: 'Starling's Law of the heart'. Simply expressed, this states that stretching the muscle fibres of the heart – by making greater demands on it – increases cardiac output up to a certain point; but beyond that point, further stretch leads to a decrease in output.

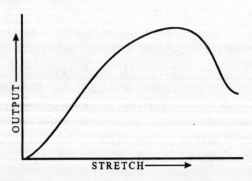

Starling's Law seems to me to embody a principle which applies to our lives. Up to a certain point, an increase in work-load increases output. But beyond this point, output falls off. There are some Christians whose output for God and for others is small because they have not allowed themselves to be stretched. They have not taken up the challenge of Christian service in Sunday School or Bible Class, or the work of a church deacon or elder. There are undoubtedly many others who are over-stretched, and living on the downward slope of Starling's curve. In this latter category, I am thinking particularly of keen, committed, middle-aged Christians who have taken on too much, and consequently do nothing effectively.

How does a state of prolonged overload come about? Are we simply the victims of our circumstances? I do not think so. I have come to the conclusion that, as a rule, those who become persistently over-busy do so by their own choice. I am not referring to temporary over-busyness. This is unavoidable. Work increases; a colleague is transferred, becomes ill or resigns and is not immediately replaced. Or management makes additional requests or demands, perhaps accompanied by an offer of an increase in salary. Such things cannot always be foreseen or avoided; or, if they are foreseen, all too often they are not acted on.

Temporary pressures are unavoidable. Persistent over-busyness, on the other hand, can, I believe, be avoided. It generally indicates a failure of judgment; and I believe its seeds are sown early in a person's career.

Personal choice

Some business and professional people choose – often subconsciously – to be over-busy. Why do they react in this way? I can think of a number of reasons. Some find their work enjoyable and fulfilling. This is certainly true of many doctors. There is the constant stimulus of diagnosis; like solving one detective problem after another.

> **Temporary pressures cannot be avoided, but persistent over-work can**

There are the remarkable recoveries. There is the gratitude of patients and relatives. There are many other jobs which similarly combine interest and variety; particularly those which involve meeting a wide range of clients. Such things are certainly more exciting than sparing time trying to help a tired wife with crying babies or difficult teenagers. So the 'worker' feels no desire to rush home.

Another reason why many people choose to be over-busy is a desire for greater prestige and the acquisition of power in the sphere of their work or, perhaps, in political life. The struggle for enhanced power (or prestige for that matter) is not necessarily wrong. It depends on a lot of factors. It depends, particularly, on whether the ambition is selfish or altruistic (see chapter 5). If a person is suitably gifted, he (or she) may be able to make a valuable contribution in these areas, from which others benefit. But it is necessary to maintain a balance and to be sure one is not neglecting the work one is paid to do and the work one has promised to do (see chapter 6).

Another reason for over-commitment, often subconscious, is that it is equated in many people's minds with importance and being indispensable. People often say to those in business or one of the professions: 'I know you are very busy,' – implying that the individual is much in demand. An aura of busyness serves as a useful defence against the call to give time to people who seek our help but whose needs are not strictly our concern or in our area of expertise.

Yet another reason for over-busyness is, of course, money. As I have already noted, it never ceases to amaze me how people will take on an extra commitment which doesn't really interest them for the sake of a bit more money which they do not really need.

There are reasons for over-busyness that are particularly relevant to Christians. There is no doubt that many are known to be 'willing horses' and therefore unlikely to refuse any request. As a result others take advantage of them. Furthermore, those in professional and business life tend to be looked up to, by virtue of their abilities and their position in society, as natural leaders in church affairs. This often involves them in additional work during the week and also erodes the day of rest.

One final reason why many Christians are over-busy is that they hold a false distinction between the sacred and the secular. Many do not recognise the dignity of their calling, and are itching to be preachers or to be involved in organising spiritual work. Most of us are called upon to display Christian character primarily by doing our work conscientiously and well, and by discharging our responsibility to our spouse and family and to society. To put overtly 'spiritual' work on a pedestal is, I believe, a fundamental and serious misunderstanding of vocation.

It would be a mistake to think of over-work as the sole, or even the main, cause of 'burn-out'. I believe disappointment and bitterness at the failure to attain a goal which at one time seemed well within our grasp are factors which are even more damaging than sheer over-work. Once our long-cherished ambition has slipped over the horizon, it is easy for a sense of frustration and purposelessness to set in.

Prevention and treatment of burn-out

How can this condition of over-stretch, leading to frustration and burn-out, be avoided? How, when we see the beginnings of it, can we extricate ourselves? No doubt it is more difficult for some than for others. There are, to my mind, two remedies. The first is to remind ourselves repeatedly that, whatever our job, we are serving Christ. Others may not think that what we are doing is important, but God does. As the poet, George Herbert, put it: 'Who sweeps a room, as for thy laws, makes that and the action fine.' Our ambition must not be to attain a particular status or achieve special recognition, but to do what God has given us to do, however humdrum, for him.

We need to know why we are where we are. Once we are convinced that God has called us to the job in which we find ourselves, however menial it may be, that is our vocation, just as much as if he had called us to teach or to preach the Gospel. It is important to remember that it was not only the prophets and priests that God used to guide his people of old. Men (and women too) in positions of leadership sometimes had the key role. One has only to think of Joseph, Deborah, Daniel and Nehemiah. Lowly jobs may have a crucial influence too. Remember the servant girl in the household of Naaman, the commander in chief of the army of Aram in the time of Elisha, the prophet. She was able to point her master to a cure for his leprosy. Remember Thomas Bilney, nicknamed 'Little' Bilney, who was able to point the great Hugh Latimer to a right understanding of the Gospel, which made him one of the pillars of the Reformation in Britain.

We need to recognise the dignity and value of work done for the glory of God. If God has called us into a particular profession or business, that is our primary task for him. Anything which contributes to that purpose is good; anything which interferes with it is bad; and anything which does not affect it is unimportant (to adapt the words of Dr. F.P. Wood).[2]

The second remedy is to be prepared to say 'No'. We must have the courage and resolve to say 'No' to money; 'No' to prestige; 'No' to power; 'No' to everything outside God's will for us.

The example of Jesus

We get the perfect example of this in the life of Jesus. His work involved tremendous pressures. The Gospels tell us that he was often thronged by multitudes of sick people and people who wanted to see him. On one occasion 'the whole town gathered at the door' of the house where he was staying.[3] On another occasion we are told that he did not even have time to eat. His friends came to take him away, forcibly, considering that his availability to all and sundry was crazy.[4] Yet his life was serene and in the highest degree effective.

146

I believe this was because he was prepared to say 'No' to requests that were outside the line of his duty. On one occasion, he was told that everyone was looking for him, but he made it clear that his work for that day lay elsewhere: 'Let us go somewhere else – to the nearby villages – so that I can preach there also. That is why I have come.'[5] He recognised his primary call as being to the Jews, and did not go out of his way to minister to Gentiles.[6]

Our Lord had a clear goal, and made everything subservient to it. He understood his mission. Making time for people was important. He also understood his own limits. He did not do

> **We must be prepared to say 'No' to demands outside the main objective of our life**

all he might have done, or go everywhere he might have gone. If he judged something to be his Father's will, he did it; if not, he refused. He knew that there were just twenty-four hours in the day, and that it was impossible for him to do everything himself, so he trained twelve assistants, whom he called apostles, and delegated specific tasks to them.

We need to be imitators of Christ, and have a clear understanding of the purpose of our lives. We should follow the Master in being prepared to say 'No' to demands outside the main objective of our life and in delegating duties which others can do – without necessarily abrogating overall direction in the first instance. Often, it is necessary to supervise and keep in touch with those to whom we delegate duties. John Wesley once remarked: 'Though I am always in haste, I am never in a hurry, because I never undertake more work than I can go through with calmness of spirit.'

One area in which I have found it particularly difficult to decide whether to say 'No' is specifically church work. I think that every child of God should be involved in some definite Christian service; but a major church commitment is in a different category. It is, in my view, not part of the primary calling of a business or professional person or a parent of small or teenage children, and requires careful consideration in the light of all the circumstances.

The importance of periodic review

It is important to review our workload and priorities periodically – at least once a year. Such a review is particularly indicated before embarking on any major additional commitment, and also at such times as illness, when the workload has to be cut. One of the pieces of advice I made a habit of giving to busy patients before discharging them from hospital was to suggest making a list of all their duties in order of their real importance: the most essential, and those which they alone could do, at the top; the least important and those which others could do just as well at the bottom. Then I advised the patient to draw a line halfway down and suggested that he (or she) should discard the lower half. This is a good exercise for every busy professional or business person to undertake periodically, and one which should not wait until health has been undermined by the bearing of burdens which we were not meant to carry.

It goes without saying that time should be used fully and efficiently. Many people waste time. It is also important to be prudent in maintaining one's health, and vigilant to avoid dependence on alcohol or drugs. Physical, mental and spiritual refreshment are essential. I used to find the occasional day spent right away from the telephone a valuable safety valve. I am blessed with a wife who has been prepared to hold the fort during these periods. Daily communion with God, and meditation on his Word are vital, however busy we are. Indeed, the busier we are, the more vital such times are. For most of us, Sunday, or a large part of it, can be both a time of spiritual renewal and a safety valve, and should be cherished as such.

There is life after retirement

Many business and professional people live as if there could be no life after retirement; whereas, with the increase in life expectancy which has occurred during the past century, many more men and women are living into the 80s and even the 90s. These post-retirement years can be a time of relaxed achievement. It is particularly a time, if health is preserved, for distilling the experience of a working life into the encouragement of young people and, perhaps, into teaching or writing. Cicero in his 'De Senectute' suggested that old men preserved their intellects if they maintained their interests.[7] It is a case of 'use it or lose it.'

References
1. Michael Jones, 'The stressed doctor in a stressful society', in *Christian Choices in Healthcare*, ed. M.D. Beer, IVP, 1995, p. 30.
2. F.P. Wood, Presidential address to the Association of American Physicians, 1966.
3. Mark 1:33
4. Mark 3:21
5. Mark 1:38
6. Matthew 15:24
7. B. Pitt, 'Social factors and old age', in *Social Psychiatry*, eds D. Bhughra and J. P. Leff, Blackwell Scientific Publications, 1993, pp.315-330.

Chapter 12

BEING AN EFFECTIVE WITNESS

'Those who have taught many people to do what is right will shine like the stars for ever and ever.'[1] There is real success for you.

Christians should be different

Jesus told his disciples that they should be like salt and light in society. 'You are the salt of the earth ... You are the light of the world.'[2] He no doubt meant that his people should act as a preservative in society and be a means of dispelling the darkness of the ignorance of God. While some members of the worldwide church have special gifts in evangelism, each of us is a witness – good, bad or indifferent – simply by virtue of the fact that we live in society, and we are watched. Remember Peter, at the trial of Jesus. The servants of the high priest did not know much about him, but they were pretty sure he had been with Jesus. One of them challenged him: 'You too were with Jesus of Galilee.' He was taken off guard and denied it.[3] He was a cowardly witness then – though later he became bold.

Christians should be different from their worldly colleagues. Some choose to express this difference by wearing a badge in the form of a fish or a dove. Wearing a cross, unfortunately, means nothing today. But the essential mark of a Christian is a distinctive attitude and life-style. The apostle Paul told the Romans: 'Don't let the world around you squeeze you into its own mould, but let God re-make you so that your whole attitude of mind is changed.'[4] Paul works this out in detail in his letter to the Christians in Ephesus. Our speech should be different: no lying, no exaggeration, no coarse joking. Our attitude to work should be different; 'doing something useful' so that we may have something to share with those who are in need. Our attitude to sexual relationships should be different; 'there must not be even a hint of sexual immorality, or of any kind of impurity.' Above all, we should demonstrate unselfish Christ-like love; being 'kind and compassionate to one another, forgiving each other.'[5] The really distinctive thing about a Christian is love, unselfish love – loving our neighbours as ourselves.

If we are known to be Christians, we are constantly being watched by our neighbours, colleagues and clients. We are like 'a city set on a hill', as Jesus put it.[6] We stand out like the 'white towns' in the landscape of the south of Spain.

Sharing the good news about Jesus

Although living a Christ-like life is to be our top priority, every Christian has the duty and privilege of speaking for Jesus, sharing with neighbours, clients and colleagues the good news about our wonderful Saviour. This is a responsibility that falls on all of us, and one for which we shall have to answer at the Day of Judgment. We should always be on the look-out for opportunities of introducing people to our greatest Friend.

When persecution arose among the early Christian church after the martyrdom of Stephen, we are told that the disciples were scattered throughout Judea and Samaria, and 'preached the Word wherever they went.'[7] As someone has put it: 'They gossiped the gospel.' This is an example for us. The apostle Paul urged his friend

> **The really distinctive thing about a Christian is unselfish love**

Philemon: 'Be active in sharing your faith.'[8] To the Christians in Colossae, he said: 'Be wise in the way you act towards outsiders; make the most of every opportunity. Let your conversation be always full of grace, seasoned with salt, so that you may know how to answer everyone.'[9] The apostle Peter said: 'Always be prepared to give an answer to everyone who asks you to give the reason for the hope that you have.'[10] We cannot know everything, but there is no justification for remaining ignorant about the basics of our faith.

Bill Hybels, the American church leader, has

said: 'There is nothing in life so exciting as befriending, loving and leading "lost" people towards faith in Christ.'[11] My own poor experience confirms this. Every new situation is big with such possibilities. It could be argued that the highest form of success is bringing people to faith in Christ and creating an atmosphere which makes it easier for them to believe in the power of God and his relevance to them as individuals.

Many Christians think of certain professions – such as medicine and teaching – as offering unique opportunities for witnessing for Christ. Those who are actually engaged in such work know that it is not as simple and straightforward as that. For example, when patients come to a doctor with physical or mental problems, it is *these* needs which must be met first. The Christian doctor must be as fully informed and as conscientious and skilful as possible. Once he has applied his medical skill to the problem in hand, then he should be available to meet spiritual need; or, more precisely, to direct the patient to where such need can be met. Aggressive Christian witness at the wrong time merely puts people's backs up. C.S. Lewis said after his conversion that too overt an attempt to convert him earlier would have been counter-productive. The caring and teaching professions undoubtedly afford special opportunities, but every profession and business affords scope for extending the kingdom of God.

It is difficult to get a right balance between living the Christian life and speaking for Christ, but most Christians would admit that too often we fail to speak when an opportunity arises. We need to remind ourselves that among those whom we meet during the course of any day, there is likely to be at least one who, unknown to us, is seeking a meaning for life, in whose mind the Holy Spirit is actively working. He is our great unseen ally.

> **Always be prepared to give an answer to everyone who asks you to give the reason for the hope that you have**

A radiologist, who was a friend of our family, used to tell how once, when he had just finished a follow-up examination of a patient he had examined many times before, the patient noticed a Bible on his desk. He stopped in his tracks and said to the doctor: 'Does this mean that you are a Christian? You've never said anything to me about it. I think you are a damned cad.' I believe the doctor rather liked telling this story against himself because it gave him a rare opportunity of using a swear word! But it challenges me to ask myself how many people I met or encountered in the course of my work could justifiably make the same complaint. Of course, we have no right to force our beliefs on those we come into contact with in our daily work. Nevertheless, our Christian faith is a tremendous help to us in our daily lives, and it would be a help to them if they embraced it.

> **The main reason why many of us find it difficult to witness is that we have not learned to be open**

John White makes the point that the main reason why many of us find it difficult to witness is that we have not learned to be open. 'We are unable to be our real selves because we are afraid. Fear seals our lips when we ought to speak, creases our faces with smiles when we are annoyed, makes us say yes when we mean no .... It is our own need to be liked that causes us by a thousand subtle gestures to deny Christ.' He goes on to say: 'A hostile reaction is to be welcomed. It may be a sign that you have prodded a sore spot.... A conversation of any kind, joking, serious, disgruntled or whatever, turns inevitably into witness if you have the courage to be yourself simply because Christ is important to you. You don't have to look for "openings": just be you.' John White gives his own experience. 'I shall never forget the morning I decided as far as possible to be simple and honest in my relationship with others.... Within an hour I was in serious conversation about Christ. And within

24 hours I had seen a man converted. I had made no conscious effort to witness or to "win a soul".'[12]

William Wilberforce, the British parliamentarian, whose labours had such a crucial effect on the ending of the slave trade, was so concerned to act as 'salt and light' in the circles in which he moved, that he used to prepare what he called 'launchers'. These were remarks designed to turn the conversation in a 'spiritual' direction. I have tried to do this from time to time, but I must confess that my efforts have shown a lack of spontaneity, and have not been noticeably effective. The main thing is that we should never lose sight of the fact that the great majority of those we meet are living in darkness and heading towards a lost eternity. We, by God's grace, have the light and the responsibility for spreading it. People with different temperaments inevitably have different approaches to witness, and often a lack of articulateness may be compensated for by evident sincerity.

What attitude is required in a Christian witness?

1. *Compassion*
We live in a hard world where the weak and wounded go to the wall. There are increasing numbers of such people today, on account of the

breakdown in families and the loss of the bond of church fellowship. The pace of life militates against gentleness and a caring attitude. In Jesus' famous story of the Good Samaritan, the priest and the Levite passed by the man who had been mugged, and did nothing to help him.[13] They had important responsibilities and were in a hurry to reach their destinations, and this took precedence over urgent human need. I find this challenging, because I am aware that I have often behaved in the same way. Time is precious and we must not waste it, but we must not schedule it so strictly that it militates against having time to help a needy person crossing our path.

2. *Sacrifice*

We are constantly urged to put our own interests first; to look after No 1. Genuine sacrifice moves people. It makes them stop and think and ask themselves: 'Why would he or she go out of their way to help me?' Of course, sacrifice involves time and money, both of which are generally in short supply; but there is no doubting its impact.

3. *Friendship*

This is undoubtedly the key to success in attracting people to Jesus Christ. We need to develop what Hybels has called: 'friendships of integrity with unchurched people.' He went on to say: 'The most authentic, compassionate and sacrificial Christians in the planet will not influence irreligious people until they make contact with them.' This, of course, involves significant amounts of time and effort, not to mention some occasional discomfort. Hybels warns against the temptation to speed up the process by introducing a specifically spiritual dimension prematurely. He has a whole catalogue of valuable suggestions for developing authentic friendships.[14]

> **Friendship is the key to success in attracting people to Jesus Christ**

I saw a splendid example in one of my senior medical colleagues. When he finished work early and had a bit of time to spare, instead of rushing home or putting his feet up and having a quiet read, as most of us did, he would stand at the entrance to his ward, greet people passing along the corridor and be available to talk with anyone who had a problem.

Ultimately, the opportunity will often come to state clearly how a person may find new life in Christ. Frequently, it comes suddenly, out of the blue, without any warning; so it is necessary to be prepared for this. Bill Hybels tells how he and his wife were on a sailing holiday, and accepted an invitation from a non-Christian couple to spend the evening with them and some of their friends on their yacht. In the course of conversation, it came out that Bill was a pastor; but there was no spiritual conversation until they were on the point of leaving. Bill was half way down the ladder into the dinghy when one of the people who had invited them said: 'Say, Bill, before you leave can you answer a question? I've always wanted to ask a Christian what it means to become one. Could you tell all of us?' Bill says: 'I knew I had their undivided attention – for about forty-five seconds – to summarize what it means to become a real Christian.'

'Well,' he said, 'first you've got to realise the difference between religion and Christianity. Religion is spelled D-O, because it consists of the things people do to try to somehow gain God's forgiveness and favour.... Christianity is spelled differently. It is spelled D-O-N-E; which means that what we could never do for ourselves, Christ has already done for us.' He went on to spell out the meaning of the death of Christ, and how we need to receive God's gift of forgiveness.[15]

We come back again to the apostle Peter's words: 'Always be prepared to give an answer to everyone who asks you to give the reason for the hope that you have.'[10] Often, the best we can do is to take the seeker to church or give them a booklet which sets out the way of salvation clearly; but such actions are only likely to be effective if they are built on a basis of respect and friendship.

160

4. *Developing the Christian mind*

If the Christian is to be effective as salt and light, he must develop his mind, in order to understand current issues in the light of God's revelation in the Bible. In this way, he can cultivate points of contact with his unbelieving colleagues. Unfortunately, few Christians have trained themselves to think outside the narrow realm of their business or professional work. Too many are afraid to think. They are uneasy when dealing with open-ended questions, and they do not see the significance of wrestling with great ideas if they cannot always come up with easily packaged answers.[16] Relatively few are equipped to challenge the assumptions of unbelievers and confront a culture which is steadily drifting away from God.

> **If the Christian is to be effective as salt and light, he must develop his mind**

An ability to think Christianly involves keeping up to date through wise selection of newspaper reading, TV, radio and films, viewing them against the background of long and deep immersion in Biblical teaching. Those brought up in a Christian home have a head start in this. Those coming to faith later in life inevitably tend to react to problems and opportunities in a non-Christian way, even though their level of commitment may put more mature Christians to shame.

Taking a stand on principle
Every Christian finds himself, from time to time, in a situation in which he feels compelled to take a different course of action from his colleagues and from what is fashionable. He has to make a stand for what he believes to be the right. How difficult this can be! Perhaps no one else sees the need for it. Even his Christian friends may not see the need as clearly as he does. He begins to wonder whether it is really necessary. The thought of being considered a prig or intolerant is repugnant.

I have never forgotten the action of a colleague of mine when we were both junior doctors in London. He was asked by his boss – one of the most powerful medical men in London – to do something dishonest. He refused point blank, saying 'It's against my principles.' The boss was enraged: 'Principles! What do you know of principles?' he stormed. But the young doctor had made his attitude clear, and it left an indelible mark on those around. In the long term it did his career no harm either.

Early in my consultant career, I was twice asked by senior colleagues to attend non-urgent conferences on a Sunday morning. I have no hesitation about undertaking acts of mercy on a

Sunday, but I could see no good reason for choosing a Sunday for a routine conference. Moreover, I could envisage the likelihood of this becoming a habit. I decided that, rather than simply declining for myself, I should argue against the practice on principle. So I wrote to the Senior Administrative Officer:

'Thank you for your invitation to this Conference. I would like to come, but I am opposed in principle to non-urgent medical meetings being held on Sundays. I fully appreciate the difficulty of finding a time which all busy doctors can manage, but doctors need a day of rest like other mortals. Those of us in clinical practice try to emphasize to our patients the need for a balanced life, and I think it sets a bad example to society when we don't practise what we preach. In addition, some doctors have commitments to the kingdom of God and to the spiritual welfare of patients on Sundays about which they do not say much, but which they nevertheless regard as being of great importance.'

The administrators tried it on once more eighteen months later; but after that the idea of Sunday conferences was dropped. Fortunately, at least in Scotland, the Christians have strong allies in the golfers, who do not like to forego their game on a Sunday morning!

Christians can act as 'salt' in relationships between management and staff, by making constructive and well thought out suggestions for the resolution of conflicts and indicating a way forward. If you feel that someone is being unfairly criticized, it may be appropriate to send him or her a personal letter of support and encouragement.

Taking a public stand

Sometimes the Christian has a duty to speak out publicly on a matter affecting the public good, by a letter to the press or to one of the professional journals. It may perhaps be a matter of business or medical ethics on which the Word of God has something definite to say. To most of us, the idea of publicity is hateful, and one shrinks from the inevitable criticism involved in putting one's head above the parapet. Then there comes to mind the famous statement of Edmund Burke: 'All that is necessary for the triumph of evil is that good men do nothing.'

Lord Fisher of Lambeth, when Archbishop of Canterbury, set down four sound rules to be observed when making a public statement:

1. Never forget that our only business is to reconcile conflicting persons and their divergent views. We may have things to say that will antagonize; but we must never say anything that ought to antagonize a fair-minded person.

2. Never use scornful or abusive words about those with whom we disagree.

3. When there is a clear Christian judgment, we should proclaim it with authority.

4. Always remember that all the facts are rarely known, and that there are at least two sides to every question.

Soon after taking up my appointment in Aberdeen, I had an experience which some of my colleagues still remember. The medical profession had just been awarded, by an independent body, what seemed to outsiders a big pay rise. Simultaneously, the Government of the day called for a period of pay restraint

> **All that is necessary for the triumph of evil is that good men do nothing**

throughout the public and private sectors. A London surgeon whom I admired, a Quaker, wrote to the British Medical Journal urging that the medical profession should give a lead to the country by deferring acceptance of their pay rise. Although my bank account was far from healthy, I felt sympathetic to the idea, and I believed that many of my colleagues, especially the Christians, would feel similarly.

Three weeks passed without a single letter in support of his suggestion; so I plucked up courage and wrote to the Journal indicating my support. By this time, the surgeon who made the proposal had written a second letter to say that he had taken the step of instructing his paymaster to withhold the increase from his own pay packet. So both our letters appeared in the same issue, but his was much more sensational than mine. Because the contents of the BMJ are released to the news agencies a couple of days prior to the date of publication, his letter made headlines in the national press before I had seen the Journal. My letter only generated local interest. But that was traumatic enough. The first I knew of the local excitement was the appearance on my doorstep of a reporter from the *Aberdeen Press and Journal* asking if I was prepared to follow the example of the London surgeon by requesting a cut in *my* pay. Having gone so far, I could hardly pull back now; so I said I would do so. This led to banner headlines in the local press the next day: CITY DOCTOR TURNS DOWN A PAY RISE – to my great embarrassment. A month later, my action was debated in the area health board – and criticized by some of the members. This led to further headlines: DOCTOR'S PAY RISE 'NO' SPLITS BOARD. I found the publicity deeply disturbing, and I think a number of my colleagues were embarrassed. On the other hand, some of my patients indicated their approval, and it did my career no harm. Contributions to the press are time-consuming and costly, but they present an opportunity of speaking up for right and for God.

Pioneering

The Christian who seeks to promote the good of the community in which God has placed him will find himself from time to time faced with an opportunity of starting some new venture. It may be organizational; such as some improvement in the running of the business or profession. Or it may be primarily spiritual; such as a special meeting for presenting our colleagues with the claims of Christ. Such an opportunity presented itself in Aberdeen, when a Billy Graham mission was relayed to a number of cities in the U.K. A similar opening sometimes occurs for starting a Scripture Union or similar group in a school in which there is, as yet, no specific Christian witness.

Any such initiative needs wisdom. It calls for prayer. It demands persistence. If it is to be effective, there will certainly be difficulties to be overcome. Any matter of Christian witness will undoubtedly be opposed by the Devil and his agents. So it is well to ask oneself at the outset: Is it really important? Is it likely to be the will of God? If the answer to these questions is in the affirmative, the objective must be defined so that it can be kept clearly in sight. Having done this, and having received confirmation that it is the will of God, one can press forward resolutely. Whenever possible, it is good to involve others and give them a part to play; always being more concerned that the objective should be achieved than about who gets the credit. When obstructions are encountered, as they surely will be, persistence in relation to the goal must be blended with flexibility as to the path by which the goal is attained.

References
1. Daniel 12:3 (TEV)
2. Matthew 5:13, 14
3. Matthew 26:70
4. Romans 12:2 (J B Phillips)
5. Ephesians 4:25–5:5
6. Matthew 5:14
7. Acts 8:4
8. Philemon 6
9. Colossians 4:5, 6
10. 1 Peter 3:15
11. Bill Hybels and Mark Mittelberg, *Becoming a Contagious Christian*, Scripture Press, 1994, p. 14.
12. John White, *The Fight*, Inter-Varsity Press, 1977, pp.67-73.
13. Luke 10:31-2
14. Bill Hybels and Mark Mittelberg, *ibid*, pp.122-153.
15. *ibid*, pp.193-202.
16. Gordon MacDonald, *Ordering Your Private World*, Highland Books, 1987, p.106.

Chapter 13

RESOURCES

'I would like to be a Christian but I couldn't keep it up.' How often do those challenged to Christian commitment say words like that. It is essential to be realistic about the difficulties involved in following Jesus. To live as a Christian in business or in one of the professions is not easy. It is like the great Tour de France cycle race. There are steep hills and deep valleys; pot-holes and slippery stretches, to be endured and negotiated, to say nothing of the jostling by other competitors. In the race of life, there are, in addition, the malign devices of the Evil One to watch out for. Success demands deep resources and persistence to the end.

To fulfil one's calling as a Christian at all adequately is impossible but for the grace of God. It means doing one's work well. It demands a life consistent with our Christian profession. And it carries with it a requirement to be ready to share our faith as occasion affords. All this calls for deep spiritual resources.

Total provision

Thank God, all the resources we can ever need are available; and this has been proved time and time again in the experience of Christians in all walks of life. The secret is learning to live day by day, and moment by moment in fellowship with God. Jesus described the Christian life in his parable of the vine as a matter of 'abiding in him', 'remaining united with him'.[1] The apostle Paul described it as keeping in step with the Holy Spirit.[2] What does this mean in practice?

Awareness of the continual presence of God is one of the most important things that this generation has lost. Our lives are filled with activity, even Christian activity, but many of us are living with little or no conscious relationship to God, who is the source of all strength and wisdom and grace. I am sure this is the reason for our relative ineffectiveness, and the fact that our labours produce such a meagre harvest. It explains why Christians are so often indistinguishable from others and achieve so little for God. It also accounts for the lack of joy and peace in our lives and in our homes. It accounts for the discouragement, the dissatisfaction, and the feeling of 'burn-out'. The resources are there in God, but they are unused; like a large bank balance which lies untouched year after year. From time to time one reads of people living in extreme poverty and hardship who actually have thousands of pounds in a bank account. Many Christians are like that.

It may be asked whether, in a busy professional or business life, it is possible to cultivate an awareness of the presence of God. In the book of Genesis, there is a lovely description of Enoch, the father of Methuselah. It says: 'Enoch walked with God.'[3] Is it possible for a doctor or a banker or a car salesman or a mother of small children in today's world to walk with God; or to say with King David: 'I keep the Lord always before me'?[4]

Awareness of the continual presence of God is one of the most important things that this generation has lost

---

Is it possible for an administrator to pray three times a day as Daniel, the prime minister of Babylon, did?[5] I believe it is, because Our Lord promised the gift of the Holy Spirit to live in his disciples. Jesus said: 'I will ask the Father and he will give you another Counsellor to be with you forever – the Spirit of truth.'[6] The Holy Spirit is called the Counsellor (also the Comforter) in the sense of a strengthener, an adviser, a helper. The promise of his indwelling presence applies to all believers. Jesus said: 'If anyone loves me, he will obey my teaching. My Father will love him, and we will come to him and make our home with him.'[7] This means that God himself lives within those who love and obey him.

The implication is momentous. It means that all God's resources are available to us. No wonder Hudson Taylor, the pioneer English missionary to China in the last century, could say: 'Think what it involves! Can Christ be rich and I poor? Can your right hand be rich and your left hand poor? Or your head well filled while your body starves?'[8] No! All the resources of God are available to his children.

The question is: How do we actually live in the experience of this? How do we keep in a state of union with Christ? The answer is – by prayer.

Prayer

Jesus taught his disciples: 'Men ought always to pray.'[9] The importance of prayer cannot be exaggerated. It is what the eighteenth century poet, James Montgomery, called 'the Christian's vital breath'. The Christian is like a diver working on the sea bed off the north-east Scottish coast. He is operating in an alien and often hostile environment, utterly dependent on his oxygen supply and telephone link. If these are impaired, he will be weakened. If they are cut, he will die. The purpose behind prayer is not selfish; it is not mere pietism. Prayer is essential if our daily service for God and for others is to be effective.

In practice, there are two sorts of prayer; there is the fixed time of prayer and there is the life of prayer.

The fixed time of prayer

I have already emphasized the importance of making a habit of setting aside time for prayer and meditation on God's Word some time during the day – ideally at the start (see chapter 6). This is so important that many years ago I invested in an alarm clock combined with a machine for preparing a pot of tea! The original contraption has long ago packed up, but I still have, at the bedside, an alarm and an electric kettle which boils the water in a little over a minute. Having wakened myself up with a cup of tea, my wife and I read a portion of the Bible and then simply talk to God; roughly following the acronym, ACTS: adoration, confession, thanksgiving, supplication. We make our own prayer list of points for supplication; praying for family needs daily, other needs weekly, and yet others monthly.

If you don't feel alert first thing in the morning, try washing and dressing before you spend time with God. It is often argued that different personality types have different patterns of activity throughout the day, so that rules of behaviour are inappropriate. Some may find it better to spend time with God in the evening, others at no fixed time. I accept that there is an element of truth in this. Nevertheless, it seems that most believers who have served God effectively in this world have adhered to a rule of life which involved spending some time with God in the morning.

William Wilberforce, who achieved so much for God through his work in parliament, wrote: 'This perpetual hurry of business ruins me in soul if not in body. More solitude and earlier hours! I suspect I have been allotting habitually too little time to religious exercises, as private devotion, and religious meditation, Scripture-reading, etc. Hence I am lean and cold and hard. I had better allot two hours or an hour and a half daily. I have been keeping too late hours, and hence have had but a hurried half hour in the morning to myself.'[10]

Having emphasized the vital importance of time spent with God, I hasten to add that no one should feel the least bit guilty about missing out this time occasionally when circumstances are exceptional.

The life of prayer

Besides the fixed time of prayer, there should be a life of prayer. Nicholas Herman of Lorraine – better known as Brother Lawrence – a lay brother in a monastic order, involved in kitchen duties, developed what has come to be called 'The practice of the presence of God'. He cultivated what he described as 'an habitual, silent, secret conversation with God'.[11] You may say: That is all right for a monk or cleric, but quite impossible for a busy business or professional person. Well, the apostle Paul did not think so. It was to ordinary working men and women that he wrote: 'Pray continually.'[12]

Often, as I set out for work, I find myself repeating, under my breath, the opening lines of Charles Wesley's famous morning hymn:

Forth in thy name, O Lord, I go,
My daily labour to pursue;
Thee, only thee, resolved to know,
In all I think, or speak, or do.

Then there are 'Nehemiah prayers' – sometimes called 'arrow prayers'. Nehemiah was a Jew in the service of the Persian king, Artaxerxes. While waiting on his royal master, the king noticed that he looked sad. The fact was that he had just received bad news from Jerusalem. On the spur of the moment, the king asked him what he could do to help. An immediate reply was expected. Nehemiah tells us: 'I prayed to the God of heaven.'[13] In the middle of his conversation with the king, he spoke to the King of kings, and received inspiration to frame an appropriate response.

Prayer is a hot line to God. Do you remember how Peter found himself sinking in the waves, and how in that instant he called to Jesus?[14] We can call to God like that.

My wife and I picked up this idea a few years ago when we were walking and talking with a friend in the open air. The name of someone in trouble came up, and our friend stopped, stood still for a moment, and simply brought the need to the Lord there and then. We have increasingly made it our practice to bring not only our own needs, but also the needs of others, to God in prayer immediately they come to our attention; perhaps whilst reading or during conversation. There is no reason why we should not speak to God on the way to a committee or a meeting with an awkward administrator, or customer or colleague. When discussing a difficult medical or personal problem with a patient or with a member of staff, I have often sent up an urgent prayer to God for wisdom and guidance.

Prayer is the most simple and natural activity

I frequently prayed before making decisions about the treatment of my patients. I remember a particular occasion when I happened to have the responsibility of diagnosing and treating a TV personality who had developed a potentially serious acute infection whilst on holiday in north-east Scotland. He clearly needed an antibiotic. There were a number of drugs to choose from, one or two of which might have been effective and the others not; and there was no way of knowing for certain which would be best. The pressure on me was greater than usual, because the illness was headline news on TV. What did I do? I prayed for divine wisdom on the basis of God's promise in the Epistle of James: 'If any of you lacks wisdom, he should ask God, who gives generously to all without finding fault, and it will be given to him.'[15] I prayed; I pondered, I prescribed – and God granted healing.

Prayer is the most simple and natural activity. James Montgomery, the eighteenth century poet, eloquently described this simplicity and naturalness:

Prayer is the burden of a sigh
The falling of a tear
The upward glancing of an eye
When none but God is near.
Prayer is the Christian's vital breath
The Christian's native air ...

One final point about petitionary prayer. I have come to believe that we should bring to God situations rather than solutions. When we are facing a problem, we can often see only one satisfactory answer and we plead for that. God, on the other hand, frequently has a better way. He usually has a surprise up his sleeve.

John White has a very helpful section on how to pray in his book *The Fight*.[16]

Reading God's Word
Another vital resource in living the Christian life is the practice of reading God's Word, the Bible, and meditating on it. In his seminar with his disciples, the night before he went to the cross,[17]

Jesus repeatedly emphasized the importance of obedience to his commands and his teaching. 'If you love me, you will obey what I command.... If anyone loves me, he will obey my teaching.'[18] We cannot obey our Master if we do not know his commands. Our Lord's teaching is primarily his own words, recorded in the Gospels. But it also includes the Old Testament, which Jesus accepted in its entirety as the Word of God[19] and from which he often quoted. The Old Testament supplies the Jewish background against which to understand Christ's words. For a proper

---

'Ten minutes spent in Christ's society every day; aye two minutes, if it be face to face and heart to heart, will make the whole of life different.'

---

understanding of our Lord's teaching, we need also to study the New Testament, which shows us how his apostles expounded and applied his words under the guidance and inspiration of his Spirit, whom he promised would assist them.[20]

The Bible imparts true wisdom. The Psalmist wrote, over 2500 years ago: 'I have more insight than all my teachers, for I meditate on your statutes. I have more understanding than the elders, for I obey your precepts.'[21] That doesn't mean that we should *know* more than our teachers in university or college. Wisdom is not the same as knowledge. A '*wise* man', says John White, 'is one who can distinguish what is fundamental from what is trivial, who knows what life is about and who acts appropriately whatever the circumstances.'[22] There is a line among the fragments of the Greek poet Archilochus which says: 'The fox knows many things, but the hedgehog knows one big thing.'[23] Many Christians are ignorant of the large stores of worldly wisdom but, thank God, they know the 'one big thing'.

The low priority accorded to the reading of God's Word is one of the greatest sources of weakness of Christians in our generation. 'Man does not live on bread alone, but on every word that comes from the mouth of God,' said Jesus.[24] Admittedly studying the Bible and meditating on it takes time; and time is a rare commodity. But we can make time for anything we regard as important. If only we realised how our lives would be transformed if we made time to wait on God and read his Word, we should find the time somehow. Professor Henry Drummond of Edinburgh once said: 'Ten minutes spent in Christ's society every day; aye two minutes, if it be face to face and heart to heart, will make the whole of life different.' One of the most important habits I learned from my father was that of reading a part of the Bible every day. No one suffers through making time in his life for God. After all, success is ultimately in God's hands.

Christians have a variety of ways of reading the Bible. Some find it best to follow a prescribed plan, with or without the help of notes. (There are many useful aids published by the Scripture Union and Bible Reading fellowships). Others read consecutively through one book of the Bible and then another, following their own inclinations. Some use both methods at different times. In recent years, my wife and I have used the NIV Study Bible, which has footnotes which answer almost all the problems of intelligibility, and the Life Application Bible, which suggests applications to contemporary living. This makes us largely independent of additional notes and commentaries. There is no set length of text to be covered. We just read as much as we have time to think about on the particular day.

Everyone gets into ruts or 'dry' periods. I certainly did. Then it is good to be able to switch to a different plan. There are audio-tapes. Some of them have a passage from the Bible. Others have a thought for the day. The important thing is to keep going with some daily exposure to God's Word; if possible before the start of the working day.

It is a good idea to ask three questions regarding each section we study. Firstly, What exactly does it say? Secondly, What does it mean? What did it mean to the author and to the original readers? Here, the footnotes in a study Bible are often a help. Thirdly, How does it apply to me, my family, my work, my neighbour and to society today? When time permits, it is helpful to compare different translations and, if possible, go back to the original languages.

When a statement in the Bible impresses me, I have found it useful to underline it, so that I can easily find it again, and remind myself of it. As we read, we must seek to obey; not like slaves, in a servile way, but as children who want to please their Father. There is a lot to be said for keeping a notebook to record lessons, and also problems. The problems can be saved up until there is an opportunity of seeking the help of a more mature Christian.

John White has a helpful section on studying the Bible in *The Fight*.[25]

Meditation

It is not enough merely to read the Word of God; we must think about it, ponder it, turn it over in our minds and come back to it again and again. I have no doubt that this is what Jesus did when he went out on the hills of Galilee before dawn. It is clear, from a reading of the Gospels, that his mind was saturated with the Scriptures. The first Psalm describes the success and prosperity that attends the one whose 'delight is in the law of the Lord' and who 'meditates on it day and night'. He is described as being 'like a tree planted by streams of water.... Whatever he does prospers.'[26]

We used to hear a lot about the value of Transcendental Meditation, and the idea is still around. Christian meditation is not the same as TM. The aim of TM is to empty the mind and produce a sense of detachment in order to improve one's psychological and emotional state. It aims to achieve relaxation and unwinding with a view to attaining a sense of inner peace and composure. Christian meditation, on the other hand, aims to empty the mind in order to fill it with an awareness of God. If we have stored our minds with God's Word, we can recall statements about God, and lift our hearts to him in praise and worship, using the words of Scripture. When we are discouraged or depressed, we can recall his wonderful promises and take them for ourselves.

We need to make time for meditation. This is not a luxury for those who are not so busy; it is an essential for effective living. It is not something for a certain type of individual – the contemplative type – but something everyone needs; something without which no one can be strong.

How can we find this extra time for meditation? Let me make some suggestions. First of all, I would suggest that we do not fill every spare moment with audiotapes, radio and TV. Many people seem unable to tolerate silence. The moment they get into the car, they switch on the radio. In the train, they listen to a tape. The moment they come home, they turn on the TV or reach for the newspaper. Let us cut down on slavery to the mass media. Then what about walking instead of going everywhere by car? It is easier (and safer) to meditate while walking. Then why not slip into a quiet place or even a convenient church for ten minutes? We must make time to wait on God.

Joining other Christians for fellowship and worship

There is one other vital resource in living the Christian life, and that is meeting together with God's people. A coal which drops out of the grate soon loses its glow and grows cold. In the same way, a Christian who neglects corporate fellowship and worship quickly becomes spiritually cold. Our Lord promised his special presence where two or three gathered together in his Name. 'Where two or three come together in my name, there am I with them.'[27] The writer of the Epistle to the Hebrews warned his readers against giving up the habit of meeting together.[28]

Many professing Christians neglect this supreme opportunity of realising God's presence. For the high pressure business or professional person, the time of corporate prayer, hearing God's Word, worship, fellowship and Holy Communion are vital. If we make this a habit, broken only when we are prevented by the call of duty, it will help us during those times which every Christian pilgrim experiences when we feel sad and discouraged, when like the Psalmist we are 'cast down and disquieted', when God seems to have forgotten us.[29] The fellowship of believers and the corporate worship of God will not only strengthen *us*; our presence will help *others* who are passing through a period of spiritual deadness.

Joining a church

You may agree that you need the fellowship of other Christians and authoritative teaching from the Word of God; but is it necessary actually to join a church? You might argue that as a believer, you are already a member of Christ's church – one with all the children of God world-wide. Why should you commit yourself to one group of believers? Why not go from place to place; like a bee sucking nectar wherever it can find it?

The first answer is that such an attitude is selfish. It is all get and no give. A church member can help the cause of Christ far more than can a casual visitor, who only gets to know his fellow-Christians superficially, and avoids becoming involved in the witness and outreach of the church.

The second reason is that it is not good for you in the long run. There will come times which are critical spiritually when you need help and support. You are far more likely to receive such support if you are a member of some church whose leaders and members know you and feel some responsibility for your welfare.

If there is more than one church within reach, which one should you join? This requires careful thought. Some join a church because others of their own age and type go there. Others because they enjoy the preaching or the liturgy. Others because it is conveniently close. Family ties are important too. But the strongest reason for joining a church is that the Word of God is proclaimed in the power of the Holy Spirit. What it boils down to basically is this question: In which of the churches in my neighbourhood shall I find teaching which is true to the living Word of God? Don't expect to find a perfect church. There isn't one. And even if there was, it would cease to be perfect once you joined it!

Students sometimes argue that all their needs are met within the Christian Union. I encourage students to throw in their weight with the CU, but the CU is not a church and it is not intended to be one. For one thing, it makes no provision for the regular obedience to the Lord's command to remember him in the breaking of bread, the Holy Communion. Moreover, the composition of the CU is not representative of the body of Christ. You miss out on the fellowship of older Christians. Many of these have learned important lessons by hard experience in the rough and tumble of life. In any case, you need to prepare for the day when you will no longer be eligible for a CU and will need a church.

Conclusion

If we are to be strong Christians, we need to take what the apostle Paul calls 'the whole armour of God', including 'the sword of the Spirit which is the Word of God' – and prayer.[30] Only in this way can we resist the onslaughts of Satan. If we are to be fruitful Christians we need, as the apostle Peter reminded his readers, to keep growing: adding to our faith, goodness, knowledge, self-control, etc.[31] And if we are to become Christ-like, which is the goal of the Christian life, we need to be constantly reminded of the example of our Lord and Saviour, Jesus Christ, of his commitment to the will of his Father expressed in his great act of submission: 'Not my will but yours be done.'[32] As a result, he is now exalted 'far above all rule and authority, power and dominion, and every title that can be given, not only in the present age but also in the one to come.'[33]

Real success is fulfilling God's purpose for your life.

Jesus is the pattern: THE SERVANT KING

References

1. John 15:4 (NEB)
2. Galatians 5:25
3. Genesis 5:24
4. Psalm 16:8
5. Daniel 6:10
6. John 14:16, 17
7. John 14:23
8. Dr. and Mrs Howard Taylor, *A Biography of Hudson Taylor* Hodder and Stoughton, 1965, p.307.
9. Luke 18:1 (AV)
10. E. M. Bounds *Power through Prayer*, Send the Light Trust, 1969, p.14.
11. Brother Lawrence, *The Practice of the Presence of God* Mowbray, 1980.
12. 1 Thessalonians 5:17
13. Nehemiah 2:4
14. Matthew 14:30
15. James 1:5
16. John White, *The Fight,* Inter-Varsity Press, 1977, pp.26-37.
17. John chapters 13–16
18. John 14:15, 23
19. John 10:35
20. John 16:12-15
21. Psalm 119:99-100
22. John White, *The Fight,* p.41.
23. Isaiah Berlin, *The Hedgehog and the Fox,* 1953.
24. Matthew 4:4
25. John White, *The Fight,* pp.39-57.
26. Psalm 1:2, 3
27. Matthew 18:20
28. Hebrews 10:25
29. Psalm 42:5, 9
30. Ephesians 6:10-18

31. 2 Peter 1:5-8
32. Luke 22:42
33. Ephesians 1:21

Wrestling With The Big Issues
Geoffrey Grogan

In this much appreciated book, Geoffrey Grogan examines the principles and methods used by Paul to assess and solve the doctrinal and practical problems that appeared in the early Christian Church. Most of these problems have reappeared throughout church history, and can be found today in evangelical churches. Geoffrey Grogan is convinced that the answers to many of today's difficulties are to be found in applying to current situations the Spirit-inspired instructions of the apostle.

Howard Marshall says about *Wrestling With The Big Issues*: 'This book is remarkable for being written by a New Testament scholar in such a simple and relevant way that any reader will be able to understand what is being said and see how Paul's letters still speak to Christians today.'

Sinclair Ferguson comments that 'Geoffrey Grogan brings to his teaching, preaching and writing a life-time of study. He combines careful exposition with practical care.'

And Clive Calver says that 'Geoffrey Grogan possesses the uncanny knack of setting truth on fire: here the personality of the apostle shines through its pages; the life of a man who Christ used to transform the history of his church.'

ISBN 1 85792 051 1   256 Pages

60 Great Founders
Geoffrey Hanks

This book details the Christian origins of 60 organizations, most of which are still committed to the God-given, world-changing vision with which they began. Among them are several mission organizations.

ISBN 1 85792 1402

large format   496 pages

70 Great Christians
Geoffrey Hanks

The author surveys the growth of Christianity throughout the world through the lives of prominent individuals who were dedicated to spreading the faith. Two sections of his book are concerned with mission; one section looks at the nineteenth century missionary movement, and the other details mission growth throughout the twentieth century.

ISBN 1 871 676 800

large format   352 pages